정

THE SPIRIT OF KOREAN CRAFT AND DESIGN

JEONG

HYO JUNG LEE

Φ

FOREWORD
BY HYO JUNG LEE
6

KOREAN CRAFT AND DESIGN: AN EVOLVING LEGACY
BY BETH MCKILLOP
8

BRIDGING THE GAP: A DIALOGUE BETWEEN OLD AND NEW
BY J KATHRYN HONG
13

CRAFT'S SUBTLE RESPONSE TO THE QUESTIONS OF OUR TIME
BY TEO YANG
16

EATING & DRINKING
먹고 마시기
18

HOUSEKEEPING & STORING
살림하고 정리하기
62

RELAXING 쉬기 110

DRESSING 입기 146

RITUAL, PLAYING & DECORATING 의례와 놀이 및 꾸미기 182

GLOSSARY 216

INDEX 218

FOREWORD

BY HYO JUNG LEE

The Korean word *jeong* resists direct translation. More than a concrete concept, it is an emotional bond that lies at the heart of Korean life, relationships and design. Encompassing deep affection and a sense of attachment, it is something that develops over time through shared experiences and familiarity. *Jeong* goes beyond love or friendship; it is an enduring, often unspoken sense of warmth and empathy that weaves together people, objects and even places.

In the context of craft and design, *jeong* is revealed through attention to detail and the profound connection between maker, object and user. It reflects a philosophy in which beauty is found not just in appearance, but also in the care and the relationships embedded in the making process. *Jeong* transforms a handcrafted object into something greater than its physical form. It represents the warmth and dedication instilled by the maker – the way in which the artisan's hands shape the materials, forging a deep respect. This emotional depth fosters a unique bond between object and owner, and one that transcends utility. From the intricate mother-of-pearl inlaid cabinets known as *jagaejang* (see page 74), to the minimalist form of the moon jar (see page 186), Korean craft tells a story of resilience, ingenuity and *jeong*.

The history of craft in Korea reflects a deep-rooted harmony between function and form, often born out of utilitarian necessity. The porous structure of the humble-looking *onggi* jar (see page 38) was designed for fermentation and storage, and its form has remained more or less unchanged for generations. Similarly, *yangeun* utensils (see page 24) – lightweight and quick to heat – were developed to be affordable and to be used daily. Over time, even the most functional objects have evolved into works of art, blending practicality with beauty and embodying the philosophy that the everyday should be meaningful.

At the heart of Korean craft lies a reverence for nature, which is regarded as the highest guiding principle in the creation of any object. Korean artisans have long believed that true beauty emerges from nature itself, and therefore often choose to work with raw natural materials in their unaltered state. This is evident in the country's rich ceramics, textiles, wooden furniture and lacquerware, in which the inherent qualities of the materials are not transformed or disguised but instead preserved and celebrated.

The objects in this volume were carefully selected to paint a broad, but by no means complete, picture of Korean craft and design. You'll find overlooked everyday objects – some shot on location in rural Korea by photographer Hyunwoo Min specially for this book – next to prized pieces from the collections of such institutions as the Onyang Folk Museum in Asan, south of Seoul, and the Victoria & Albert Museum in London. The ubiquitous rubber gloves (see page 71) found in almost every Korean kitchen sit alongside exquisite *norigae* (see page 158) woven from delicate horse-hair. A gauzy shade (see page 116) of *mosi* – a fabric crafted from ramie, the nettle-like plant native to East Asia prized for its breathability – appears in the same chapter as a monumental bed made from a slab of stone (see page 137) that is believed to offer health benefits. Each object has a story to tell and traces a lineage from the ancient to the searingly modern. You'll find a glossary of Korean terms and list of key periods and dates on page 216.

More than a survey, this book is both a celebration of Korean craft and an invitation to experience Korea through its design traditions. These objects imbued with *jeong* continue to shape the texture, rhythm and intimacy of Korean life.

KOREAN CRAFT AND DESIGN: AN EVOLVING LEGACY

BY BETH MCKILLOP

From the tenth to the twentieth century, Korea was ruled by just two dynasties: the Goryeo (918–1392) and the Joseon (1392–1897). The capital of Goryeo was Gaeseong, located centrally on the peninsula. This era was marked by deep devotion to the Buddhist faith. Temples flourished, artisans carved woodblocks for printing sacred *sutras*, and agriculture prospered. Successive waves of war and invasion brought metalworkers and potters from China, who often shared their techniques with Korean craftspeople. These migrants introduced refined methods of decorating vessels and working in bronze. The royal court and aristocratic families commissioned elegant jade-green ceramics known in Korea as *cheongja* – and in the West as celadons – which were used both for formal dining and in scholars' studies.

Following a prolonged period of civil unrest in the fourteenth century, Korea reasserted its sovereignty as Mongol control waned. The Joseon Dynasty was founded by Yi Seong Gye, who took the title Taejo and established Seoul (then known as Hanyang) as the new capital. Despite the turbulence of the Japanese invasions in the 1590s and the Manchu campaigns of the 1630s, the Joseon Dynasty ruled without interruption for more than five centuries. Joseon society was grounded in the teachings of Chinese philosopher Confucius and adhered to a rigid social hierarchy. At the top were the *yangban*, the elite ruling class, who monopolised government positions. They were followed by a small class of *jungin* (literally, 'middle people'), while the majority of the population consisted of commoners, primarily farmers. At the base of the hierarchy were *cheonmin*, 'vulgar commoners' or the lowborn. The *cheonmin* carried out occupations that were deemed impure or despicable – such as butchery, execution and entertainment – and were legally and socially segregated from society. Many artisans, including potters, belonged to this lower class. Women had limited social standing and were largely excluded from public and intellectual life, expressing their creativity instead through domestic crafts.

Korean visual and material culture reflected these hierarchical values. Educated elites, trained in Chinese artistic traditions, were schooled to admire paintings that embodied Confucian ideals: landscapes, bamboos and pines, or scenes with literary associations. Art forms linked to the lower social classes were often dismissed as inferior. When Korea began to open to foreign powers in the late nineteenth century, such aesthetic distinctions influenced early Western scholarship. Academics and collectors accorded privilege to the material culture of the elite, relegating objects associated with daily life to the realm of 'craft' or 'decorative arts'. However, since the 1980s, as South Korea's contemporary art scene has flourished, this hierarchy has increasingly been challenged. Today, artists, scholars and collectors engage critically with these inherited divisions.

Contemporary Korean makers reimagine traditional forms with originality and ambition. Potters craft monumental jars inspired by historical *onggi* storage vessels (see page 38), while a host of tailors, designers and couturiers reinterpret the cropped *jeogori* jackets (see page 167) and flowing *chima* skirts of the classic *hanbok* once worn by married Joseon-era women. Craft lies at the heart of all artistic production. Skill, aesthetic instinct and design knowledge converge in the creation of every object, and boxes, vessels, garments and jewellery continue to be shaped by Korea's long and evolving design legacy.

Hanji, Korea's traditional handmade paper, has been produced for over 1,200 years. The process involves soaking the inner bark of trees, rags or straw in cold water, adding mucilage from hibiscus root to disperse the fibres, and straining the mixture through a bamboo frame before air-drying. Fine, long-fibred *hanji* was made for royal calligraphy, while coarser grades were used for bureaucratic and educational purposes. Papermaking is seasonal, as low temperatures are essential for tightening the fibres and inhibiting bacterial growth. *Hanji* was produced in various forms for books, floor and window coverings, and decorative applications, while twisted paper fibres, when oiled and waxed, became a durable material for small-scale furnishings.

The lustrous black ink used by printers and artists was made from charcoal and stored in solid form. Brushes, fashioned from animal hair inserted into bamboo or wooden handles, were prepared with great care by skilled artisans. Every book, whether printed or handwritten, reflected the collective labour of authors, woodblock carvers, ink-makers, papermakers and binders; each decision, from thread type to the placement of stab holes, guided by tradition and craft.

Among the most celebrated legacies of Korean craft is its ceramic tradition. Stoneware and porcelain kilns operated nationwide throughout the Goryeo and Joseon periods. Although the names of most potters are lost to history – not recorded in the copious historical records that survive from court and regional magistrates' offices and in the libraries of distinguished families – their sophisticated works endure in museum collections. Some of the most refined celadon wares were created in the eleventh and twelfth centuries for Buddhist tea rituals. Jade-green glazes adorned bowls, ewers, incense burners and water droppers, many shaped as animals or mythical creatures. One remarkable incense burner takes the form of a seated lion grasping a ball, mouth agape to release scented smoke (see page 190). Another stands on rabbit-shaped feet beneath an intricately pierced sphere sitting on a lotus flower with outspread petals. These pieces, prized for their luminous glazes and sculptural forms, demonstrate technical mastery and creative exuberance.

Goryeo potters adapted methods from Chinese kilns but developed distinctly Korean styles. They pioneered *sanggam*, an inlay technique using dark and light clays. A thirteenth-century Chinese connoisseur, Taiping Laoren, declared Goryeo celadon 'first under heaven' – a singular accolade, especially from a culture that typically viewed its own artistic achievements as supreme. Following the fall of Goryeo, Joseon potters developed new techniques and styles, including *buncheong* ware, which was characterized by white slip decoration, stamping, iron-oxide painting and carving (see pages 46 and 48). These expressive, tactile wares are now seen

as emblematic of Korean ceramic identity. Many *buncheong* and porcelain tea bowls were exported to Japan, where they were valued highly in tea-ceremony culture.

Joseon white porcelain reflected the austere values of a Confucian state, its colour aligning with ideals of purity, simplicity and virtue. Court rituals and seasonal ceremonies required a wide array of bowls, cups, jars and ewers. Away from the halls and pavilions of the palaces, delicately painted blue-and-white wares were more common. The most iconic forms were tall jars decorated with dragons, but pieces depicting cranes, carp or such auspicious characters as *su* (longevity) and *bok* (happiness) also proliferated. This porcelain was admired by Sōetsu Yanagi, founder of Japan's *mingei* movement, who described its aesthetic as possessing a 'beauty of sadness'. Others see in it a mood of warmth and quiet joy.

In Korean domestic interiors, the natural world was ever present. Paper-covered window frames could tilt or slide to filter light and air. Underfloor *ondol* heating enabled floor-based living, where meals were taken from small wooden tables known as *soban* (see pages 56, 57 and 58), which could be stored away after use. Chests and boxes housing clothing and bedding (see page 75) could be plain or adorned with metal fittings or lacquer. Mother-of-pearl furniture (see page 74), once reserved for royal use, Buddhist temples and court circles, later became a symbol of elite domestic taste. The visual interplay between mother-of-pearl and the black or red lacquer base – applied meticulously in layers – was central to the refinement of these courtly furnishings. Lacquer, a hard, water-resistant coating made from the toxic sap of trees in the genus *Toxicodendron*, protected wooden surfaces and allowed intricate embellishment with tortoiseshell, twisted wire or inlaid shell; popular designs included floral scrolls and idealized landscapes. Craftspeople also prized such native woods as zelkova, persimmon and maple, often burnishing them with oil to a warm sheen. Boxes and chests were assembled carefully using animal glues, strengthened with decorative nails and metal fittings.

Joseon domestic architecture reinforced Confucian gender roles, which dictated that men and women should have separate quarters in the home. In a traditional Korean upper-class home, women lived in the *anchae* (inner quarters), where they cooked, sewed and raised children. Men occupied the *sarangbang*, or study, where they read, wrote poetry and entertained guests. The Confucian ideal of self-cultivation shaped the rhythms of the gentleman's life: reading classical texts, writing poetry, and preparing for the national civil-service examinations that governed access to office. Although most women were excluded from formal education, a few learned to read and write and became noted artists and authors.

Given the Confucian gentleman's devotion to self-cultivation, every object he handled was expected to reflect his scholarly refinement. Even his attire conveyed rank and virtue. When outdoors, he wore a black *gat* (see page 151) – a hat woven from horsehair – enclosing his topknot and secured with a tight headband. Court officials dressed in formal robes for royal audiences, their bureaucratic rank signalled by *hyungbae* (see page 178): embroidered badges depicting birds or animals alongside such motifs as rocks, clouds, waves and the mythical *pullocho*, or plant of eternal youth. These badges were stitched in damask silk, sometimes lined with mulberry-bark paper. Embroiderers added depth through padded stitches and textured patterns.

Beyond the court, embroidered accessories, such as purses and spectacle cases, attested to the skill of female artisans. Wrapping cloths known as *bojagi* (see page 98) were fashioned from silk or cotton, embellished with embroidery, printed designs or patchwork. Pillow ends (see page 119) were adorned with vibrant circular plaques in ceramic, lacquer or mother-of-pearl, featuring such motifs as phoenix couples with chicks or auspicious Chinese characters, offering symbolic comfort. Elsewhere in the home, screens (see pages 114 and 209) provided both decorative enrichment and protection from draughts, or served as portable backdrops for family gatherings.

Although the secluded, self-sustaining society that once supported Korea's craft traditions has largely vanished, the spirit of making endures. Across urban studios and rural ateliers, contemporary Korean artisans continue to draw on traditional materials, techniques and aesthetics. Trained jewellers, potters and designers cater to a growing urban middle class, while family-run workshops – often operating against considerable financial odds – persist in producing handmade paper, lacquered vessels, indigo-dyed cloth and coiled-clay storage jars. Together, these practices bear witness to a cultural legacy rooted in deep material knowledge and an enduring reverence for the handmade.

BRIDGING THE GAP: A DIALOGUE BETWEEN OLD AND NEW

BY J KATHRYN HONG

As Korean culture gains global prominence, Korean crafts are receiving increasing recognition internationally for their richness and diversity. They embody both individual expression and communal identity, playing a crucial role in transmitting cultural heritage. The rising profile of Korean crafts and design invites a deeper understanding of Korean culture itself. But what is it about Korean craft that continues to speak so powerfully to makers today?

Korea's history is long and rich. Throughout shifts in ideology, religion and philosophy, the one constant has been the land itself: the Korean Peninsula, with its mountainous terrain and four distinct seasons. Even after the Japanese occupation and the Korean War (1950–53), Koreans rebuilt on the same ground, entering a period of industrialization and eventually establishing the Republic of Korea. The region's topography and climate shaped a way of life marked by adaptability, restraint and connection with nature. These values are evident in the quiet elegance of Korean forms, in the subtle tension of straight lines and gentle curves, and in the blurred boundaries between human life and the natural world.

Such sensibilities are deeply embedded in Korean aesthetics, permeating all aspects of daily life, from food and clothing to domestic space. They are particularly evident in the field of craft, where artistic intent meets technical skill to create objects for daily use. Unlike fine art, which is often contemplative or symbolic, crafts are made to be handled, worn and lived with. In their very use, they reflect the culture, environment and historical moment from which they emerge.

The Loewe Foundation Craft Prize – created by former creative director of Loewe, Jonathan Anderson, to celebrate excellence in modern craft – was awarded in 2022 to Dahye Jeong (see pages 97, 158 and 200), the first Korean recipient of the prestigious international award. Jeong works in horsehair, a traditional material once used for making *gat* (see page 151) – the traditional hat worn by Korean gentlemen. Finer than thread yet highly elastic, horsehair is well suited to forming delicate but resilient structures. Jeong's vessels, the forms of which resemble ancient ceramics or woven baskets, possess an organic presence and quiet strength. Their translucency belies the painstaking labour required to produce them. Her recognition for 'reviving tradition with creative artistry' brought encouragement to Korean craftspeople, especially as horsehair craft has become nearly obsolete.

Other Korean finalists for the Loewe Foundation Craft Prize include Sungho Cho (see page 197), who trained in metalwork and jewellery and works with delicate sheets of silver; Suk Keun Kang (see page 102), who hand-carves wood into meticulous shapes and champions the *ottchil* technique, applying approximately thirty coats of naturally heated lacquer to his pieces;

Hyejeong Kim (see page 191), a ceramicist who reshapes wheel-thrown vessels by hand to create sculptural pieces that she likens to blossoming flowers or ripened fruit; Inchin Lee, who explores the chance effects of fire in wood-fired kilns and expands ceramics into spatial installations; silver inlay specialist Sunyi Shin; and metal artist Yeunhee Ryu, a 2025 finalist. Their work attests to the breadth and innovation of contemporary Korean craft. Many of these artists maintain long-standing collaborations with Arumjigi and Onjium – two organizations that are instrumental in sustaining and reinterpreting Korean material heritage. While Korea's domestic craft market remains limited, international biennials, fairs and awards offer vital platforms for Korean makers. These events often emphasize innovation rooted in tradition, a principle that aligns closely with the missions of Arumjigi and Onjium.

Founded in 2001, Arumjigi – its name a Korean term meaning 'to protect and nurture the beautiful' – is a not-for-profit organization dedicated to safeguarding and revitalizing Korean cultural heritage. Although designs that connect tradition and modernity have become the trend, when Arumjigi was first established at the turn of the twenty-first century, tradition was often viewed negatively. It is true that Korea's unique cultural values were neglected during the Japanese colonial period, the division of North and South, and the subsequent period of economic growth. At a time when high efficiency and growth were essential, people considered traditional food and craft cultures outdated, and thought they should be discarded. Arumjigi's founders began not with fixed plans but with a shared question: what could be done to recover and revalue the elegance embedded in traditional ways of living?

One of the organization's first projects was the renovation of a modest *hanok* (a traditional Korean house) to demonstrate how traditional architecture could be both beautiful and functional in modern life. Arumjigi also undertook preservation work at palace sites, including Changdeokgung, Deoksugung and Gyeongbokgung (all in Seoul).

In 2011 Arumjigi proposed a new approach to historic architecture, one based on active use rather than static preservation. In collaboration with designer Jihoon Ha, they installed contemporary furniture rooted in traditional forms, hosting educational programmes and events in reanimated palace interiors. Ha's designs – among them aluminium Naju Bansang tables with lacquered finishes – were later included in the Korean Heritage Room at the Cathedral of Learning, University of Pittsburgh, USA, where they continue to serve students. Since 2015 Arumjigi has led efforts to re-create furnishings for historic palaces. These projects breathe life into empty interiors, making traditional aesthetics tangible once more. The foundation's earliest shows challenged the idea that tradition belongs only in museums. Instead, crafts were exhibited in *hanok* settings, freed from display cases, inviting viewers to imagine them in daily use. Although unconventional at the time, this approach fostered a renewed intimacy with traditional objects – not as relics but as companions.

Workshops held during the preparation of these exhibitions encouraged deep collaboration across disciplines. This spirit led to the founding in 2013 of Onjium, a cultural research institute and craft school focused on the realms of food, clothing and housing. Onjium encompasses three interconnected studios: a *hanbok* (traditional clothing) atelier, a kitchen dedicated to Korean cuisine, and a *hanok* design workshop. It is a place of making, research and education, where traditional techniques are advanced through study and experimentation.

Onjium's curriculum weaves together philosophical, literary and historical study, fostering both technical mastery and critical reflection. The goal is not simply to preserve tradition, but to interpret and adapt it, creating objects that are both functionally relevant and aesthetically resonant in contemporary life. Through this approach, Onjium articulates a vision for Korean craft that is both rooted and responsive, ensuring that its cultural depth continues to inform and enrich daily experience.

Both Arumjigi and Onjium were founded to provide a model of cultural stewardship that treats tradition not as fixed or frozen in time, but rather as a living foundation for contemporary life. Korean crafts endure not only through preservation, but also through reinvention, being reanimated by makers who look to the past with imagination as well as reverence. The quiet beauty of Korean objects – their restraint and harmony – continues to speak to our present condition, offering an alternative to the transient and the disposable. In this ongoing conversation between old and new, Korean craft finds a fresh voice, sustaining a lineage of care, thought and embodied knowledge – and reminding us that tradition can continue to shape the present and inspire the future.

CRAFT'S SUBTLE RESPONSE TO THE QUESTIONS OF OUR TIME

BY TEO YANG

Long woven into the quiet rhythms of daily life, craft is now being reconsidered as a means of expressing meaning within contemporary culture. No longer confined to purely utilitarian or ornamental forms, it offers a subtle yet compelling response to the challenges of modernity. In the wake of rapid industrialization, tradition was displaced by efficiency and standardization, and the tactile intelligence of the human hand was gradually eroded. Yet it is precisely at the brink of this loss that we are drawn back to the values embedded in tradition and the significance of place. This rediscovery echoes earlier cultural moments, such as the Arts and Crafts movement led by William Morris or the functional modernism of the Bauhaus – both born of similar crises of value.

Craft is increasingly understood as a vessel for time, place and culture. Ways of life and aesthetic sensibilities formed over generations have taken material shape through it, tangible forms carrying intangible heritage. Here, locality is more than a geographical condition; it becomes a sensory and interpretive language, offering alternative modes of connection. In this way, craft, shaped by hands rooted in place, reveals what mass production and digital abstraction have dulled.

Ultimately, craft is not simply the making of objects; it is a reflective practice that reclaims human sensitivity and creative agency. It invites slowness, depth and a reconnection with embodied experience. Craft moves not at the pace of the machine, but with the warmth of the hand. It becomes a bridge linking human and natural, past and future. Such gestures offer more than aesthetic value; they propose new possibilities for emotional, ethical and relational ways of living.

The potential of craft also lies in its response to the pressing concerns of our time: sustainability, cultural continuity and care. In an era of excess – overproduction, overconsumption and ecological disruption – craft offers another way of orientating ourselves. Its gestures are quiet but insistent, constituting an invitation to live with attentiveness, to recentre the knowledge of the hand and to honour ways of life grounded in material care. These practices do more than preserve memory; they reconfigure it for the present. They suggest a path towards social relationships and ways of sensing the world that are slower, more reciprocal and ultimately more sustainable.

These ideas find particular resonance in Korean craft, which, eschewing ornamentation, is marked by restraint, modesty and an aesthetic grounded in use. It moves fluidly between function and spirit, between the everyday and the artistic. Such artisanal practices as metalwork, lacquer, woodworking and ceramics reflect an ethos of precision and respect for both material and maker. These are not merely inherited techniques but modes of attention that honour the intrinsic properties of natural materials and the quiet vitality of process. More than objects, Korean craft offers a form of cultural continuity, a living record of gesture, skill and communal memory sustained across generations.

At the heart of Korean traditional crafts lies an aesthetic ideal shaped in the late Joseon period: the philosophy of *mumi*, or 'beyond beauty'. Closely intertwined with the sensibilities of Korean craft, *mumi* values a beauty stripped of artificial ornament, one that seeks essence and arises from harmony with nature. This harmony is not mere imitation of natural forms, but rather a distillation of the spirit and order inherent in the natural world, expressed through the language of craft. Artisans worked with, rather than against, the character of their materials, deliberately avoiding excess decoration. Instead, they pursued a unity in which function and form merge without force. In this way, Korean craft objects transcend the role of tools. They become quiet works of art, infused with the maker's touch and the spirit of their time. These are works in which restraint is not emptiness, but a space where meaning deepens, allowing beauty to be encountered in its most unadorned and essential form.

Now, as we look to Korea's traditional crafts, we are led to ask: what have we lost, and what must we now recover? What can the sensitivity of the hand offer our shared future? Korean craft answers these questions not through assertion but through practice, offering responses embedded in process, in care, in continuity.

Craft, in this light, is not only a way of making, but also a way of thinking. It gathers threads of time, place and experience, imagining new configurations for living. As this book shows, Korean artisans continue traditional practices while reinterpreting them in dialogue with the present. Within their work are sensibilities and ethics that resonate far beyond the objects themselves.

May this book serve as a gentle invitation to reflect on the role of craft in contemporary life. More than an archive, it is intended as a space for thoughtful dialogue and shared perspectives on the evolving significance of Korean craft. In doing so, it gestures towards the quiet yet enduring relevance of making, and the futures that might yet be shaped by the hand.

EATING & DRINKING

먹고 마시기

EATING & DRINKING

Korean society is, at its heart, shaped by food; the way Koreans eat reflects the way they live. Mealtimes gather family and friends, and the most meaningful conversations often unfold over shared dishes. Indeed, when Koreans greet one another, they don't ask 'How are you?' but rather, '*Bap meogeosseo*' or (more formally) '*Jinji deusheotseoyo*' – 'Have you eaten?'

To host someone for a meal at home is a gesture of affection in Korea, yet a Korean feast is never solely about the food. Equal attention is given to the vessels in which it is served and the utensils with which it is eaten. Tableware is selected with great care, not simply for aesthetics, but also for purpose. Many of the objects found on a Korean table arose from practical needs, the choice of materials and techniques refined to preserve heat, keep dishes cool or support the process of fermentation.

Korea's food culture is also profoundly shaped by the country's pronounced seasons. The shift from searing summer heat to bitter winter cold dictates not only what is eaten, but also how it is served. In the winter, stews and bone broths arrive bubbling in *ttukbaegi*, traditional earthenware that retains heat. A sizzling *dolsot bibimbap* must be served in a stone bowl (see page 22), designed to form a golden crust of rice at the bottom – *nurungji* – that is scraped up and savoured at the end as a sweet finish. By contrast, the summer brings cold dishes, such as *naengmyeon*, served in *bangjja yugi* bowls (see page 25) – hand-forged bronzeware that keeps its contents chilled. This seamless harmony between food, season and vessel speaks to a culture that is deeply attuned to nature, where meals are crafted not only to nourish, but also to resonate with the world outside.

Korean culinary traditions also place great value on the vessels that are used in the preparation of food. These carefully crafted objects are integral to the making and maturing of food itself, as well as to the act of eating. Earthenware *onggi* jars (see page 38) have long been used to ferment such staples as kimchi, *gochujang* (red chilli paste), *doenjang* (soybean paste) and soy sauce. Available in a wide range of sizes – from small household jars to large containers capable of storing months' worth of fermented foods for restaurants – *onggi* have been part of Korean life for more than two millennia. They were developed in an era before refrigeration, and remain remarkably effective. Coated in a natural glaze made from powdered earth and water, *onggi* are fired at a low temperature, preserving their porous texture. This porousness allows carbon dioxide to escape during fermentation, encouraging the growth of lactic acid bacteria and supporting the transformation of raw ingredients into complex, preserved flavours. *Onggi* are best stored in a cool place; traditionally, they were buried in the ground to maintain a stable temperature throughout the changing seasons.

Economy, too, has shaped the development of everyday kitchenware. Many utensils were born out of necessity, made from materials that were inexpensive or readily available. Although less common today – in part owing to concerns about the release of toxins – *yangeun naembi*, aluminium pots with a distinctive golden hue, have been a fixture in Korean households since the 1960s. As the country shifted from an agricultural to an industrial society, and the light metal industry grew, these simple anodized pots gained popularity for their lightness and excellent thermal conductivity. They became particularly associated with cooking *ramyeon*, the beloved noodles found in every corner of the country. The same aluminium is also used to make small bowls for drinking *makgeolli*, a lightly sparkling rice wine once enjoyed mostly by elderly farmers. In recent years, the custom has returned with new energy, and *yangeun* bowls (see page 24) can now be found in stylish bars across Korea. Many connoisseurs insist that *makgeolli* tastes better when it is served in this way.

Koreans are undoubtedly particular about food. This attentiveness may be a lingering echo of the trauma that followed the Korean War, when parents' most urgent concern was often whether their children had eaten. Today, to eat well – to eat nourishing, high-quality food, and to uphold the rituals and materials that surround it – carries profound cultural meaning. In this chapter, we explore the beauty of the natural lacquer techniques that preserve timber tableware, the hand-forging of brass that gives *yugi* its warmth and weight, and the enduring ceramic traditions whose roots lie in fourteenth-century craft, yet remain vibrantly relevant today.

DOLSOT | ANONYMOUS | STONE

Soup and broth-based dishes are essential to Korean meals, and they are believed to lose both flavour and texture once they go cold. For this reason, serving food at the right temperature is seen as a sign of care, attentiveness and respect. The *dolsot*, meaning 'stone pot', is typically made from natural stone and retains heat exceptionally well, allowing individual servings of soup or stew to remain hot. In such dishes as *bibimbap*, the *dolsot* also creates a prized crispy crust of rice at the bottom of the vessel, to be savoured at the end.

돌솥

FROSTED-GLASS BOWL | SEUNG YEON LEE | 2025 | GLASS

Seoul-based glassmaker Seung Yeon Lee combines delicacy with practicality in everyday vessels. Her frosted-glass bowls feature a tactile matte finish that gently diffuses light, reflecting the quiet simplicity of her work.

반투명 유리그릇

YANGEUN | ANONYMOUS | NICKEL SILVER

Yangeun, a nickel-silver alloy, became common in Korean households in the mid-twentieth century. Lightweight, affordable and durable, it replaced earlier metalware and became a fixture in modern kitchens. It was often used for bowls and lunchboxes, and also became the standard material for cups serving the traditional Korean rice wine *makgeolli* (pictured). Today, its retro aesthetic evokes memories of rural life and post-war Korea.

양은

BANGJJA YUGI BOWL | ANONYMOUS | BRONZEWARE

Bangjja yugi is traditional Korean bronzeware, forged through repeated hammering to achieve both durability and a soft golden lustre – *yugi* refers to the copper-tin alloy, while *bangjja* denotes the hammering technique. *Yugi* also has natural antimicrobial qualities. Once reserved for royalty and the elite, such bowls were valued for their ability to retain temperature, keeping soups hot in winter and dishes such as *naengmyeon* (cold-broth noodles) cool in summer. Today they remain a refined and sustainable presence on the Korean table.

방짜유기 그릇

GUP | ANONYMOUS | BRONZEWARE

This pedestal dish, or *gup*, is also made of *yugi*, the bronze alloy of copper and tin. The raised base is not simply for presentation; in Korean culture, elevating food honours and expresses respect towards the person being served. Such dishes were central to *jesa* (ancestral rites) and festive occasions, where rice cakes, fruit and delicacies were presented with solemn dignity.

유기굽

CHANHAP | GEE JO LEE | PORCELAIN

These tiered food containers designed by Gee Jo Lee reinterpret the elegant simplicity of the Joseon-era white porcelain known as *baekja*. Korean dining is renowned for its abundance of side dishes (*chan*), and *chanhap* (see also pages 30 and 42) offered an organized and portable way to serve them. Stackable and lidded, they preserved food from contamination, while saving space on low tables. Their portability also made them ideal for outdoor settings.

찬합

BUNCHEONG TEAPOT WITH PEONY DESIGN | SANGWOOK HUH | 2020 | CLAY

Buncheong is a form of stoneware developed in the fifteenth century, identifiable by its decorative use of white slip on dark clay. Patterns are created by carving, stamping or painting into the surface. Ceramicist Sangwook Huh continues the tradition in his Seoul studio, hand-carving peony motifs into this teapot using *bakji*, a sgraffito-like technique that reveals contrasting layers of clay.

티팟

AGALMATOLITE KETTLE | ANONYMOUS | JOSEON DYNASTY | AGALMATOLITE

Carved from dense agalmatolite, this kettle retains and distributes heat evenly, making it particularly suited to herbal teas and medicinal brews. The stone absorbs heat slowly and releases it gently, so it allows liquids to remain warm without scorching. It withstands gradual changes in temperature and can endure for decades. With its cylindrical body, straight spout, angular handle and fitted lid, this kettle combines practicality with refined craft. Such kettles were cherished kitchen heirlooms in the regions where agalmatolite was quarried.

곱돌주전자

CHANHAP | ANONYMOUS | JOSEON DYNASTY | BAMBOO, LACQUER

The *chanhap* (see also pages 27 and 42) is a tiered food container, Korea's traditional equivalent of today's lunchbox. This example, made of bamboo and finished with lacquer, stacks neatly, each layer holding a different food, such as rice, side dishes or sweets. A cord handle secures the tiers for transport, making it ideal for keeping food fresh on journeys. During the Joseon period, such containers were used for picnics, day trips, or delivering treats to relatives and honoured guests.

찬합

UNMUN BOWL AND PLATE | SANGIN KIM | 2015 | PORCELAIN

These pieces by Sangin Kim (see also pages 33 and 93) reinterpret the traditional Joseon white porcelain. The small dessert plate is inspired by the form of the *wonban* table (see page 57), while the companion lidded noodle bowl recalls the intimate scale of *bosigi*, small vessels once used for side dishes. Both feature a decorative cloud pattern carved into the foot – *unmun* is Korean for 'cloud'.

운문면기

SOKURI | ANONYMOUS | BAMBOO, STRAW

소쿠리

The *sokuri* is a shallow, wide basket woven from bamboo or straw, an essential household tool in traditional Korea. Its open weave allowed air circulation and drainage, making it ideal for washing rice or beans, drying vegetables and grains, and sorting harvested produce. Its shallow rectangular form was practical for spreading foods out to dry or sort.

GOJOK JEOPSI | SANGIN KIM | 2017 | PORCELAIN

Sangin Kim (see also pages 31 and 93) is known for reinterpreting Joseon ceramics with refined originality. His porcelain often carries a subtle bluish tint, produced by the iron content of the clay and revealed through traditional firing methods. The hue, embodying clarity and restraint, has taken years of experimentation to achieve. Kim has played a pivotal role in popularizing the *gojok jeopsi* (high-footed dish), a form once reserved for ritual and banquet use.

고족접시

LOW LIDDED BOWL | JONG DUK LEE | BRONZEWARE

낮은 그릇

Created by Jong Duk Lee (see also opposite and page 88) – a master of the *bangjja* metalworking tradition – this large lidded bowl reflects a continuation of Korean hammered bronzeware techniques. Based in Seoul, Lee is credited with producing the majority of Korea's *bangjja* objects. His practice requires precise control of temperature and hammering; the metal must be removed from the furnace at the correct moment and hammered for the optimal duration to achieve the desired shape and durability.

SPOON AND CHOPSTICK SET | JONG DUK LEE | BRONZEWARE

Forged by repeated heating and hammering, *bangjja yugi* bronzeware (see also opposite and page 25) is made from a dense alloy of copper and tin, producing durable utensils with a distinctive matte lustre. During the Joseon Dynasty, such brass spoons and chopsticks were favoured by royalty and the elite as a symbol of refinement and status. They are still widely used today.

방짜유기 수저 세트

CUP WITH HANDLE | ANONYMOUS | THREE KINGDOMS PERIOD | STONEWARE

This rare handled cup from the personal collection of Teo Yang dates from the Three Kingdoms period and strikingly anticipates the modern mug. Such pieces were produced mainly in Gaya and Silla between the fourth and sixth centuries; they are unusual in early East Asian ceramics, and it is possible that they were influenced by Greco-Roman prototypes. Although simple in form, this example reveals a refined sculptural sensibility. Fired at over 1,000°C (1,830°F) in climbing kilns, the durable stoneware rings with a metallic tone when struck.

손잡이 잔

KI | ANONYMOUS | BAMBOO

The *ki* was once one of the most common grain sieves (or winnowing basket), found in nearly every rural Korean household. Typically shallow and scoop-shaped, it was woven from bamboo or wicker and held in both hands to toss grains into the air, naturally separating the husks from the seeds through movement. Because of its hat-like form, the *ki* was also associated with a playful, if embarrassing, folk custom whereby children who had wet the bed were sent around the village to ask neighbours for salt or rice, wearing the *ki* on their head to hide their face. 키

ONGGI | ANONYMOUS | CLAY, SAND

The *onggi* is Korea's iconic earthenware jar, known for its porous, breathable structure that makes it ideal for fermenting such foods as *kimchi* and *gochujang* (red chilli paste). Made from iron-rich clay mixed with sand, it is fired at a relatively low temperature, creating a semi-permeable surface and giving the *onggi* its signature breathability. Originally developed before refrigeration, it allowed food to be stored safely for long periods. Archaeological evidence indicates that comparable clay storage vessels were in use on the Korean Peninsula as early as the Three Kingdoms period, with antecedents traceable to prehistoric times.

옹기

JEOLGU | ANONYMOUS | STONE

The *jeolgu* is a large mortar, traditionally made of stone and paired with a long wooden pestle known as *gongi*. Still found in the rural countryside, it is used to grind and pound grains and seeds by hand. The *jeolgu* often appears in children's books as a symbol of communal effort, especially in the making of *tteok* (Korean rice cakes), which had to be pounded by groups of people before such holidays as Chuseok or Lunar New Year.

절구

MAETDOL | ANONYMOUS | STONE

The *maetdol* is a traditional stone mill for the grinding of grains, beans and seeds – all ingredients central to Korean cooking – and was commonly used to make soybean paste. Before electricity reached rural areas, the *maetdol* was essential in many households and although less common today, it is still used in many markets and homes.

맷돌

GAMASOT | ANONYMOUS | CAST IRON

A large cast-iron pot traditionally placed over an *agungi* (wood-fired furnace), the *gamasot* was commonly found in the kitchens of *hanok*. Incredibly durable and versatile, it was used for everything from boiling rice to simmering stews and steaming grains, and was often passed down through generations as a treasured family heirloom. The *gamasot* served not only to cook meals, but also to heat the home. As firewood burned beneath it, the heat and smoke travelled through flues beneath the floor before exiting through the chimney, naturally warming the stone floors of the house.

가마솥

THREE-TIERED CHANHAP | IL WOONG KIM | 2009 | BRONZEWARE

Portable containers were used during the Joseon Dynasty by scholars and travellers to carry freshly cooked rice and side dishes outdoors. This contemporary three-tiered *chanhap* container (see also pages 27 and 30), made from *yugi* (see page 25) – a material valued for its natural antibacterial properties – reflects that tradition. Each layer holds rice, desserts or side dishes separately, keeping the flavours distinct.

삼단 찬합

LIDDED BOWL WITH TWO HANDLES | SUN TAE KIM | 2009 | BEECH VENEER

Another contemporary interpretation of the *chanhap* (see opposite), this piece is made from beech veneer by designer Sun Tae Kim, who is known for reimagining traditional Korean vessels through a minimalist lens. His work emphasizes clean geometry, subtle textures, and harmony between material and form. This example features smooth, integrated handles, making the vessel easier to hold and carry.

두손잡이 찬합

SANGBO | ANONYMOUS | RAMIE

The *sangbo* is a traditional square cloth used to cover food. Made from silk, *mosi* (ramie) or *mumyeong* (cotton), it served a practical purpose: to protect food from dust, insects and dirt as it was carried from the kitchen to the dining room, often across a courtyard in a *hanok*. *Sangbo* also helped to retain warmth and contain aromas before a meal was served.

상
보

WHITE PORCELAIN BOTTLE | ANONYMOUS | JOSEON DYNASTY | PORCELAIN

This octagonal porcelain bottle, made in the eighteenth century, reflects a form that was much admired by Joseon potters. The vessel would have begun as a rounded body that was later pared back to create flat, angular planes. On each of its eight sides appears a different floral motif – including chrysanthemum, daylily, bamboo, orchid and plantain – each brush-painted in cobalt-blue underglaze. Such bottles resonated with the ideals of the *yangban* elite, who valued purity, uprightness and simplicity.

백자병

BUNCHEONG BOTTLE WITH PEONIES | ANONYMOUS | JOSEON DYNASTY | CLAY

Dating from the fifteenth century, this flask was made using the *buncheong* technique, a method by which vessels are dipped in white slip clay and often decorated with folk motifs, such as peonies or fish. Crude in form, with a coarse surface, *buncheong* wares were typically made by and for the working class using dark, iron-rich clay, which gave the pottery its uneven texture. The coating of white slip was applied to mask imperfections, and simple, expressive designs were incised or painted on to the surface. What began as a practical approach developed into a distinctive aesthetic that continues to influence Korean pottery today.

모란 분청사기 편병

OVAL BOTTLE | KANG HYO LEE | 2014 | CLAY

Kang Hyo Lee, widely regarded as one of the leading ceramic artists of his generation, has work in the permanent collections of the Metropolitan Museum of Art in New York and the Victoria & Albert Museum in London. Renowned for his ability to fuse contemporary forms with traditional decorative techniques, he produces both monumental vases and smaller-scale vessels, including jars and teapots. This oval bottle exemplifies his contemporary interpretation of the *buncheong* technique (see opposite).

타원형병

BOSEONG DEOMBEONGI TEA BOWL | GI JIN SONG | 2015 | CLAY

Boseong Deombeongi is a distinctive type of *buncheong* ware (see pages 28 and 46), characterized by vessels coated or dipped in white slip to create a luminous white surface. Emerging in the late fifteenth century, during the early Joseon period, the production process involves a meticulous three-firing technique. *Deombeongi* vessels are particularly prized for drinking tea, since the iron-rich clay is believed to soften the bitterness of the drink. This tea bowl by contemporary ceramic artist Gi Jin Song showcases the revival of the style.

보성 덤벙이

WHITE PORCELAIN BOTTLE | ANONYMOUS | JOSEON DYNASTY | PORCELAIN

This white porcelain bottle is believed to have come from Gwangju, a region renowned during the Joseon Dynasty for its delicate white porcelain, known as *baekja*. From the late fifteenth century onwards, the Joseon royal court established official kilns there, producing ceramics that were prized for their simplicity and restraint as a reflection of Confucian ideals. These kilns, known as *bunwon*, continued to operate until the late nineteenth century, crafting wares that embodied the aesthetic values of the era.

백자병

CHAEBAN | ANONYMOUS | BAMBOO

The *chaeban* is a traditional Korean tray, an essential household tool for preparing or serving food. It was made by weaving thin bamboo strips into a grid pattern, providing a sturdy yet breathable surface that allowed air to circulate. Lightweight yet durable, it could be used to drain water from noodles or blanched vegetables, or to cool freshly fried foods, such as *jeon* (pancakes), letting the excess oil drip away. The tight weave of the strips ensured that food would not fall through the gaps.

채반

CHAESANG | SIN JEONG SEO | BAMBOO, LACQUER

This exquisite piece crafted by Sin Jeong Seo is a black-lacquered *chaesang* (see also page 108), a basket designed for storing and carrying tea ceremony items or tableware. The lid can also be used as a serving tray. Historically cherished by noble families and included in bridal dowries, *chaesang* were both functional and profoundly symbolic. Each box, lined with luxurious paper and trimming, reflected months of skilled labour. Sin Jeong learned the craft from her father, Han Gyu Seo, the second-generation *chaesang* master.

채상 바구니

HANGARI | ANONYMOUS | JOSEON DYNASTY | PORCELAIN

This porcelain *hangari* (jar) is decorated with loosely painted birds in flight, rendered in copper-red underglaze. Although copper pigments had been employed on Goryeo celadon as early as the twelfth century, they were not widely used in Joseon ceramics until the mid-eighteenth century (this piece likely dates from 1700-1850). The pigment was notoriously unstable, requiring precise firing conditions, and often yielded uneven tones and blurred outlines, as seen here. While contemporary Chinese kilns were producing vibrant polychrome wares, Korean potters avoided such lavish palettes, which conflicted with the restrained Confucian aesthetics of the Joseon court.

항아리

OIL BOTTLE | ANONYMOUS | GORYEO DYNASTY | STONEWARE

During the Goryeo Dynasty, small stoneware bottles like this one were commonly used to store scented oils and cosmetic treatments, such as hair oils. This example, dating from the early twelfth century, features a thick brown slip beneath a crackled celadon glaze. The pattern is thought to represent sprays of foliage.

기름병

HAP | ANONYMOUS | JOSEON DYNASTY | VARIOUS MATERIALS

The *hap* is a traditional Korean lidded vessel used in both daily life and ceremonial contexts. It was usually brass but could also be made from celadon, porcelain, bronze or silver, and in a domestic setting it was used for serving warm foods, such as noodle soup, rice-cake soup, rice and steamed dishes. By the mid-Joseon period, the *hap* was common among the *yangban* elite and ordinary households alike. It was also used in *jesa* (ancestral rites), where it contained sacred offerings, embodying the idea of safeguarding and treasuring what lay inside – whether food, ritual offerings or symbolic gifts.

합

TTEOKSAL | ANONYMOUS | CERAMIC

The *tteoksal* is a stamp used to imprint decorative patterns into the surface of the rice cakes (*tteok*) integral to ritual offerings and celebratory feasts. Carved from hardwood or formed in ceramic, as this one is, the reliefs traditionally carried auspicious motifs that were unique to each household. The act of imprinting beauty on to food expressed both hospitality and reverence, elevating the humble rice cake to a bearer of symbolic meaning.

떡살

MAJOKBAN (SOBAN) | BYUNG YONG YANG | 2024 | AILANTHUS WOOD

In the Joseon Dynasty, upper-class Koreans often dined on individual wooden tables known as *soban*, rather than gathering around a communal table. These lightweight trays were carried from the kitchen and placed on the floor for meals. Over time, *soban* developed into a diverse craft tradition, with many regional styles distinguished by their proportions, leg shapes and uses. Today, they are still used throughout Korea as multipurpose tables, writing desks or small altars. This piece by renowned craftsman Byung Yong Yang is in the *majokban* (tiger-legged) style, so named for the curved, tapering legs that splay outwards like the paws of an animal.

마족반

WONBAN (SOBAN) | BYUNG YONG YANG | 2020 | WALNUT WOOD

Artisan woodworker Byung Yong Yang (see also opposite) has built his reputation on the craft of *soban*. This version – a *wonban*, or round table – is turned from a single piece of wood using a lathe. Once used simply to serve food, such tray-like forms now serve many roles in the home.

원반

JISEUNGBAN (SOBAN) | ANONYMOUS | JOSEON DYNASTY | HANJI

Jiseungban is a type of *soban* crafted using *jiseung*, the art of twisting and weaving narrow strips of *hanji* paper into cords. The cords form the body of the table, and the structure was often reinforced with pasted paper or lacquer for durability and resistance to water. Lightweight and functional, such tables were used to carry and serve food, tea or alcohol. In the late Joseon period, both craftsmen and scholars practised *jiseung*, as did women making everyday items. The craft was so widespread that there are records of books being stolen from noble households because of the high value and short supply of paper.

지승반

SIDE TABLES WITH SMALL FACETS | YONG JIN CHUNG | 2021 | STAINLESS STEEL

By welding together geometric strips of laser-cut stainless steel, artisan metalworker Yong Jin Chung crafts a modern reinterpretation of the *soban*. Trained in metalwork and jewellery, Chung has developed a practice that merges industrial metal processes with 3D and digital technologies.

사이드 테이블

SAMBAL | YESL LEE | 2024 | WOOD, LACQUER, LEATHER

Seoul-based designer Yesl Lee (see also pages 114 and 117), in collaboration with Onjium's design department (see page 14), created the *Sambal* table, a contemporary reinterpretation of a compact tripod table depicted in ancient Goguryeo tomb murals. These murals, dating from the fourth to seventh centuries, offer vivid portrayals of daily life, including scenes of hospitality and ceremony, where such low tables were commonly used. The top of this example is crafted from wood and finished with a lacquered leather surface, combining traditional materials with modern aesthetics.

삼발이

YEOT SCISSORS | ANONYMOUS | STEEL

These scissors are used to cut *yeot*, a Korean confection made from rice syrup. This sweet can take many forms, from soft liquid to hard taffies or candies. The scissors cut the *yeot* into small pieces and also serve as a tool to hammer it down on a wooden board so that it does not move. Beyond their practical use, they are recognized for their distinctive sound, reminiscent of castanets, when the blades snap shut. This noise attracts customers, and *yeot* sellers often entertain crowds through their cheerful singing and deft, rhythmic movements of the scissors.

엿가위

HOUSEKEEPING & STORING

살림하고 정리하기

HOUSEKEEPING & STORING

Korean attitudes towards tidiness and cleanliness are deeply rooted in Confucian ideals, which have shaped the rhythms of domestic life since the Joseon Dynasty. A clean home was understood as a reflection of a clean mind; an ordered space suggested serenity, clarity and emotional balance. It was not uncommon for households to clean daily, wiping floors by hand and folding laundry with care. Diligence in maintaining order was praised as a virtue, and the tidiness of one's home was considered a matter of family pride and social standing.

This ethic of order extended beyond the home into personal conduct, embodied in the figure of the *seonbi* – the Confucian scholar. The moral backbone of traditional Joseon society, the *seonbi* was defined not by wealth or power but by virtue, moral integrity and the relentless pursuit of learning. For the *seonbi*, cleanliness held profound meaning; it signified respect both for oneself and for others. Even when living in rural poverty, these scholars maintained clean fingernails and polished shoes; their humble homes, although simple, were uncluttered and precise, reflecting inner clarity and disciplined living.

The *seonbi jeongsin* (*seonbi* spirit) endures in Korean society today, shaping ideals of self-discipline and dignity in labour. Within this world view, cleaning is not considered menial but honourable. Washing clothes, sweeping floors and tidying the home are gestures of integrity and respect. This sensibility informs long-standing customs: deep-cleaning before hosting guests, as an expression of care, and seasonal cleaning before major holidays, such as the Lunar New Year. These practices are more than practical routines; they are rituals of renewal, moments of transition that symbolize letting go of the old to make way for the new.

Personal hygiene is equally valued. Historically, bathing was a communal practice, and public bathhouses were integral to everyday life. These spaces were not designed for leisure but for rigorous cleansing, which could be achieved more effectively in the bathhouse than at home. Here, the *ttaesugeon* (see page 72), a coarse exfoliating towel, was essential. After soaking in hot water, the skin was vigorously scrubbed to remove dead cells. More than a matter of hygiene, the act of exfoliation carried a symbolic weight; it was imagined as a way to shed toxins, fatigue and stress, leaving the body and mind renewed. The *ttaesugeon* remains beloved today, not only for its unrivalled efficiency, but also for its symbolic function: a tool for shedding, both material and emotional, and beginning again.

This pursuit of cleanliness and efficiency extends to the design of domestic objects. Among the most iconic is the Korean *gomujanggap*, the bright pink rubber gloves ubiquitous in Korean households (see page 71). Designed for durability and resistance to heat, they have become cultural symbols of tireless care. Their presence speaks to an ethic of meticulousness in the domestic sphere, where hygiene and order are held paramount.

Within these carefully maintained interiors, storage objects reveal a dialogue between necessity and craft. Korea's shifting climate – humid summers, harsh winters – demands vigilance against mould, dust and damp. Traditionally, handwoven grass boxes were used to store bedding, garments and household goods, their earthy texture and simple geometry embodying a connection to nature and craft. Bamboo boxes, light yet strong, offered breathability and seasonal adaptability, balancing practicality with quiet beauty. Then there were the *jiseungham*, braided paper cord boxes made through the ancient art of *jiseung*, using *hanji* (traditional mulberry-bark paper). Once crafted from leftover newspapers, the strands were twisted by hand and woven into resilient containers for storing jewellery, documents and keepsakes. These materials brought lightness and sustainability to the home – stackable, adaptable, and harmonizing with the low furniture of traditional Korean interiors.

Not all storage, however, was purely functional. *Jagaejang*, lacquered cabinets inlaid with mother-of-pearl (see page 74), were once treasured fixtures in Korean bedrooms. Their surfaces shimmered with motifs of cranes, clouds and peonies, while inside lay neatly folded *yo* – the quilted bedding for sleeping on the floor – safeguarded from dust and sunlight. These cabinets were more than furniture; they became cultural heirlooms, vessels of memory passed from one generation to the next.

Together, these practices and objects form a material language of care. In Korea, a clean, ordered home is not mere appearance; it is an ethic, a gesture of respect to oneself, to family, and to those who enter. Outward tidiness reflects inner clarity. In this space of harmony, the home becomes not only a shelter, but also a mirror of the mind.

PPALLAEPAN | ANONYMOUS | WOOD

Before washing machines, clothes were scrubbed clean using the *ppallaepan*, a grooved wooden board. Its design maximized friction without damaging the fabric. Laundry days were communal, with women gathering to wash, talk and share news at the river or well with their *ppallaepan*.

빨래판

BITJARU | ANONYMOUS | GRASS, STRAW, STRING

This traditional form of broom, known as *bitjaru*, was commonly found in rural Korean households and remains in use today. Made by bundling dried grasses or twigs and tying them tightly with string, this simple tool was often homemade or purchased from local craftsmen. Keeping entrances and pathways clean was a sign of respect, so the *bitjaru* was typically placed near the front gate.

빗자루

GALDAE BITJARU | DONG KYUN LEE | 2022 | COMMON REED

Dong Kyun Lee is dedicated to preserving the traditional Korean craft of broom-making. His workshop in Jecheon, Gwangdeok Broomcraft Studio, is one of the last in the country still producing brooms using ancestral methods. These techniques include harvesting *galdae* (reed), boiling it in salt water and binding it by hand – a meticulous process passed down through generations of his family.

갈대 빗자루

MYEOKSEORI | ANONYMOUS | STRAW

Myeokseori, a tightly woven straw container traditionally found in rural Korea, is used to store and transport crops, as well as to dry threshed grains. Its dense weave ensures that not a single kernel of harvested barley or millet is lost. Typically rectangular at the base, the *myeokseori* is produced in various sizes and can last for several years, making it a durable and readily accessible tool.

멱서리

PARICHAE | ANONYMOUS | PLASTIC

The *parichae* is a plastic fly swatter, typically found hanging in the kitchen or by the front door. Before fly screens were common, insects frequently entered homes during Korea's hot summers, and the flexible handle and mesh head of the *parichae* made it an efficient and affordable tool for swatting them away. Mass-produced from the 1960s onwards, the *parichae* was soon to be found in nearly every home. For many people, it also carries a humorous sense of nostalgia – the playful threat of unruly children being swatted by elders to keep them in line.

파리채

GOMUJANGGAP | ANONYMOUS | RUBBER

These bright rubber gloves – *gomu* means rubber, and *janggap* means gloves – are a familiar sight in Korean kitchens. Designed specifically for dishwashing, they are long and thick, protecting hands and arms from hot water and detergent. Dishwashing machines were introduced relatively late in Korea, and many households still prefer to wash dishes by hand, believing it to be more effective.

고무장갑

TTAESUGEON | ANONYMOUS | VISCOSE

These brightly coloured exfoliating cloths are among the most iconic tools of Korean bathing culture. Made from rough viscose, they are used to scrub away dead skin after soaking in hot water. Bathing has long been a communal ritual in Korea, with families often visiting public baths together. Parents would scrub their children, and older children would in turn care for elderly parents – a gesture of affection and intimacy that turned routine hygiene into an act of familial bonding.

때수건

DAEYA | ANONYMOUS | PLASTIC

Before indoor plumbing became widespread in Korea, washing and bathing often took place outside. During the 1970s, large brown *daeya* basins became a household essential. Made from lightweight, inexpensive plastic, they were typically placed near outdoor taps and used for washing faces, bathing children, rinsing laundry or cleaning dishes. Today, this humble yet iconic object evokes strong memories of rural village life. 대야

JAGAEJANG | ANONYMOUS | JOSEON DYNASTY | LACQUER, MOTHER-OF-PEARL

자개장

The *jagaejang* is a cabinet decorated using the art of mother-of-pearl inlay, in which thin slices of shell – most commonly from abalone or pearl oysters – are cut by hand and set into lacquered wood. Common motifs include flowers, birds, butterflies and cranes, and each piece is carefully embedded and sealed beneath layers of natural lacquer, creating a dark, lustrous surface with a distinctive sheen. Refined during the Joseon Dynasty, these cabinets were produced by highly skilled artisans. They became symbols of wealth, taste and refinement, and were often given as part of a bride's *honsu* (dowry). Many families still treasure them as heirlooms.

SAMCHEUNGJANG | ANONYMOUS | JOSEON DYNASTY | WOOD, BRASS

As homes became more structured in the late Joseon Dynasty, specialized furniture emerged. The *samcheungjang*, or three-tiered chest, was created to store clothing, bedding, documents, valuables and other household items. Constructed with three stacked compartments, each fitted with hinged doors, it was often made from fine woods, including Chinese mahogany, zelkova or pine. They symbolized wealth and refinement and were prominently placed in the women's quarters (*anbang*) of the home. The brass fittings (*duseok*) reinforced the structure while adding decoration, often featuring motifs such as bats (representing fortune) or lotus flowers (purity).

삼층장

SPLIT | SHINKYU SHON | 2019 | PINE WOOD, STAINLESS STEEL

Shinkyu Shon's *SPLIT* series fuses traditional Korean craft with contemporary industrial design. Each piece juxtaposes split pine logs – historically used in *hanok* construction – with mirror-polished stainless steel. The contrast between the crisp geometry of the metal and the wood's irregular grain produces sculptural works that speak to the cultural dualities shaping Korea today.

분절

JIGE | ANONYMOUS | WOOD, ROPE

In a mountainous country with a long agricultural tradition, Korean farmers needed a practical way to transport heavy loads along narrow paths and across hills and valleys. The *jige* – a wooden frame worn like a backpack, secured with rope and supported on the shoulders and back – was developed as a solution. Pre-dating the Joseon Dynasty, the *jige* was once used to carry everything from firewood to harvests, with people often bearing loads over 50 kg (110 lb). Although now less common, the *jige* is still used in rural Korea, particularly in hilly or forested areas, to carry cut grass or branches.

지게

CHAEKJANG | ANONYMOUS | JOSEON DYNASTY | WOOD, LACQUER

The *chaekjang* was a specialized storage cabinet for books, documents and scholarly materials, typically found in a scholar's study (*seojae*). In the Confucian society of Joseon Korea, books represented not only knowledge, but also moral cultivation and refinement, and for the *yangban* elite, owning a well-crafted *chaekjang* was a mark of education and prestige. This example, naturally lacquered, features a grid-like arrangement of small drawers to organize and protect books, and intricately carved legs that raise the piece off the ground.

책장

SABANGTAKJA | ANONYMOUS | JOSEON DYNASTY | WOOD

The *sabangtakja* – literally 'four-sided table' – is a narrow wooden display shelf open on all sides, designed to be appreciated from every angle. It was used to display celadon, books or lacquerware objects that reflected the family's cultural and intellectual identity. In Confucian society, where refinement and scholarship were highly valued, carefully arranging objects on a *sabangtakja* expressed both taste and knowledge. These shelves were smaller and lighter than most cabinets, and could be moved around easily.

사방탁자

DAENAMU BAL | ANONYMOUS | BAMBOO

Daenamu bal (woven bamboo blinds) were traditionally hung in windows, doorways or open thresholds during Korea's hot summers, forming a screen that shaded the interior while allowing a breeze to pass through. To make them, bamboo – a fast-growing and readily available material – was split into thin strips, smoothed and bound with cord. These lightweight, portable screens could be rolled, stored or moved with the seasons. Beyond cooling the home, they also served to divide interior spaces while preserving airflow and the diffusion of light.

대나무발

HAEJU HANGARI | ANONYMOUS | JOSEON DYNASTY | STONEWARE

Hangari (jars) such as these were produced in Haeju, Hwanghae Province (in present-day North Korea), in the late nineteenth and early twentieth centuries. Crafted from durable stoneware and used to store rice, condiments and other foodstuffs, they combine the scale of traditional storage jars with the solidity of porcelain. They are decorated with bold underglaze brushwork in cobalt-blue, iron-brown and green, often featuring fish, peony or cloud motifs drawn from folk painting, and reflecting the lively, expressive aesthetic of *minhwa*. While part of the late Joseon ceramic tradition, they are less delicate in form and finish than the refined white porcelains that were produced at the royal kilns.

해주 항아리

HANDWOVEN HANJI BASKET | YOUNG MI PARK | 2024 | HANJI

Historically, scraps of paper were recycled into household items through *jiseung*, a technique that involved cording, and then tightly weaving, strips of *hanji* into remarkably durable objects, such as baskets, fans and boxes. Today, Young Mi Park is one of few remaining artisans preserving this labour-intensive method. The process begins with soaking and sun-drying the paper more than fifteen times before the weaving starts – a task that can take up to two months to complete by hand.

한지 바구니

DAMYANG BAMBOO OBJECTS | ANONYMOUS | BAMBOO

Damyang, often called Korea's bamboo capital, has cultivated and woven bamboo for centuries, producing household tools, storage boxes and ceremonial objects. Bamboo grows vigorously in the region, enduring four distinct seasons that make it stronger and more resilient than bamboo from other parts of the country. Crafting begins with carefully selecting three-year-old bamboo, which is then split into fine strips and smoothed to remove splinters. The strips may be dyed with natural pigments or coated with lacquer for beauty and durability, and are then woven into intricate patterns without the need for nails or glue.

담양 대나무

JI-CHANG | EUNGBOK CHANG | WOOD, HANJI

Ji-Chang is a contemporary reinterpretation of the traditional 'breathing cabinet' used for food storage during the Joseon Dynasty. These cupboards employed *hanji* paper, silk or linen to cover wooden frames, allowing ventilation. Eungbok Chang's modern version contrasts a simple wood-and-paper exterior with colourful silk panels inside, painstakingly hand-painted with traditional motifs.

지장

STACK | JAEWOO AHN | 2023 | ASH BURL, BRASS

The Korean folk tradition of *doltap* involves stacking stones to make a wish. Drawing inspiration from this ritual, Jaewoo Ahn's *Stack* cabinet features wooden volumes containing concealed drawers, each crowned with a bronze handle cast from a real pebble. These knobs are intentionally textured and designed to grow smoother with time and touch, echoing the way stones are gradually shaped by the elements.

돌탑장

WOVEN LEATHER CASE | DAHYEON YOO | 2023 | LEATHER

These leather cases were the first original designs by Dahyeon Yoo (also known as Debaroun). After working as a digital effects artist in the film industry, she took a year-long global journey. The diverse craft traditions she encountered on her travels deepened her appreciation for Korea's native artisanship. Upon her return, she took up leathercraft before enrolling in formal courses in traditional Korean straw and grass craft at the Pulzip Craft Museum in Gwangju, where she mastered weaving and plaiting techniques dating back to the Joseon Dynasty. Yoo reinterpreted these methods to create the intricate outer straps of these vegetable-tanned leather boxes.

땅콩 초배기 가죽함

HANDWOVEN BAMBOO BAGUNI | HEE WOO | 2024 | BAMBOO

Every winter, Hee Woo journeys to Damyang – a southern town famed for its bamboo forests – to gather materials for his craft. There, he selects and cuts stalks of *wangdae* bamboo, which he dries in the sun for several months. These are then woven by hand into robust, practical pieces, such as trays, baskets (*baguni*) and boxes.

대나무 바구니

BANGJJA BOWL | JONG DUK LEE | 2024 | BRONZEWARE

Jong Duk Lee (see also pages 34 and 35) crafts his bowls using *bangjja*, a thousand-year-old Korean technique of metalworking dating back to the Goryeo Dynasty (see also page 25). Molten metal is poured into a mould, then hammered into shape while still red-hot – a method that produces distinctive strength and resonance.

방짜유기 그릇

BRASS STOOL | HYUN SUNG KIM | 2019 | BRASS

The son of a metalworker, Hyun Sung Kim was introduced to the discipline at an early age. After graduating from art school, he established his own practice, focusing on refined tableware. This brass stool marks his first venture into furniture design – a series of functional seats made using traditional metalworking techniques, elevated by precise detailing. The piece can also be used for storage.

황동 스툴

DADEUMI BANGMANGI | ANONYMOUS | WOOD

Dadeumi bangmangi are traditional laundry bats that were used in pairs to beat freshly washed clothes and fabrics. Struck alternately, the bats smoothed out wrinkles and softened fibres. Since most garments – including *hanbok* – were made of cotton, hemp or ramie, this beating process replaced ironing. The distinctive percussive rhythm of *dadeumi* work resonating from courtyards and riverbanks became a familiar sound across Korea.

다듬이 방망이

GRAIN CABINET | KIM, KWON, YOO | 2018 | WALNUT WOOD, HANJI, OLED

This walnut cabinet is a collaboration between designer Eun Hak Kim and carpenter Won Deok Kwon (see also page 125), the latter a master of *somok*, a traditional Korean joinery technique that relies on precise hand-cut joins without nails or glue. They were joined by Bae Geun Yoo, Korea's last remaining *hanji* paper screen-maker. Repurposed as the cabinet's panels, Yoo's *hanji* screens are gently illuminated from within by an OLED, its soft light revealing the delicate grains and textures of the paper and wood.

결

SQUARE TEA BASKET | BAMGUREUM (BORAM KIM) | 2025 | BAMBOO, WOOD

Each winter, Boram Kim (see also page 99) travels to the bamboo groves of Damyang to harvest materials for her finely woven designs. Crafted by hand at her home in Yangpyeong-gun, this basket was created for tea breaks on the move. It is designed to carry pots and cups, and features a wooden lid that doubles as a small tabletop or tray.

팔각사각차바구니

SMALL HAP | SANGIN KIM | 2024 | PORCELAIN

Sangin Kim (see also pages 31 and 33), reinterprets Korea's ceramics heritage with refined simplicity, drawing inspiration from Joseon Dynasty white porcelain. This *hap* (see also page 54), a lidded container for food, jewellery or precious objects, includes an inner lid decorated with blue peonies, symbolizing prosperity, honour and abundance. The double cover provides extra protection and expresses the cultural belief that valuable objects should be safeguarded materially and symbolically. Since 2012, Kim has run the brand Haeinyo, creating vessels for everyday life through experiments with clay, glaze and form.

작은 합

BLESSING POUCH | SEONG IM JEON | 2019 | ABACA FIBRE

Bokjumeoni are drawstring pouches believed to carry good fortune. This contemporary rendition was made by Seong Im Jeon (see also page 109), director of the Pulzip Craft Museum in Gwangju, who has been experimenting with weaving and basketry for more than 35 years. The piece uses a fabric made from fibres of the abaca (Manila hemp) plant – native to the Philippines. Jeon embellished the surface with delicate, hand-stitched details in thread.

복주머니

SAEKSILNUBI PINCUSHION | JUNG HOON LEE | 2015 | SILK, COTTON, HANJI

Pincushions (*banul bangseok* or *banuljip*), usually made from cotton or silk and stuffed with cotton or wool, prevent pins and needles from rusting and provide safe storage. They have been used in Korea for centuries. More elaborate forms, called *chimnang*, were made from silver or horn, and embroidered silk versions could be worn as decorative accessories. Often attached at the waist, they allowed women to keep needles at hand. This contemporary version is by Seoul-based textile designer Jung Hoon Lee, who uses a traditional Korean quilting technique known as *saeksilnubi*.

바늘방석

SEWING BOX | ANONYMOUS | JOSEON DYNASTY | MOTHER-OF-PEARL

Najeon-chilgi is a form of Korean lacquerware inlaid with pieces of mother-of-pearl from abalone, turban and pearl oyster shells. For more than two thousand years, it has been a refined expression of Korean craft. The technique – *najeon* – is thought to have been introduced during the Three Kingdoms period from Tang Dynasty China. The beauty, lustre and durability of the objects made them favoured gifts to the royal court. Mother-of-pearl trays were commonly used to serve tea or the traditional Korean confectionery known as *hangwa* and the technique was also used to make exquisite sewing boxes such as this open-topped example.

자개 반짇고리

A TIME OF SINCERITY | DAHYE JEONG | 2022 | HORSEHAIR

Delicately handwoven from horsehair, the basketry of Dahye Jeong (see also pages 158 and 200) draws on a technique used during the Joseon Dynasty to craft *gat* (see page 151), the wide-brimmed hats worn by Korean nobility. The process is intricate and lengthy; fine strands of hair are threaded around a wooden form using needles, then heat-treated before the core is removed, revealing the final woven shape.

성실의 시간

BOJAGI | HOHODANG | 2025 | RAMIE

The origins of the *bojagi* – wrapping cloth – are uncertain, but it is thought to have arisen from the need to carry and protect belongings. Typically square in shape and made of silk, ramie or cotton, it was used to wrap, store and transport objects. In daily life, *bojagi* covered food and household items, while in more formal settings it enveloped gifts and ritual offerings. The act of wrapping carried symbolic meaning, expressing respect, protection and the wish for good fortune. At weddings and rituals, brightly dyed *bojagi* conveyed blessings. A play on words deepened its resonance: the Chinese character *bok* (cloth) was pronounced the same as *bok* (good fortune).

보자기

FLORAL LATTICE TRAY | BAMGUREUM (BORAM KIM) | 2023 | BAMBOO

A trained woodworker, Boram Kim (see also page 92) began experimenting with bamboo after moving from Seoul to the rural area of Yangpyeong-gun. Initially seeking a basket for her garden produce, she taught herself to weave using locally harvested materials. This piece, a *chaeban* (traditional serving tray), is finely woven in a floral lattice pattern using delicate bamboo strips.

꽃살문 바구니

SILVER INLAID VESSEL | ANONYMOUS | JOSEON DYNASTY | IRON, SILVER

This traditional vessel – used to hold water, incense, or ritual offerings – is decorated with fine silver inlay, known as the *eun ipsa* technique. Fine grooves were carved into the surface, filled with silver wire, and hammered smooth, creating shimmering geometric textures that lie flush with the surface. Silver was associated with purity and thus lent symbolic weight to vessels used in ancestral rites. Such works reflected not only technical mastery, but also cultural refinement, and ownership of a piece like this signalled high social status.

은입사 수로

HWAGAKAM | ANONYMOUS | JOSEON DYNASTY | WOOD, OX HORN

This vivid red storage box is decorated using *hwagak*, a traditional Korean craft in which slices of ox horn are ground into a paper-thin translucent veneer, reverse-painted with motifs and fixed to a wooden surface. The luminous quality of the horn enhances both the red background and the intricate designs. *Hwagak* boxes could be used to store valuables, such as jewellery and documents, as well as sewing tools, cosmetics and keepsakes.

화각함

OTTCHIL WOODEN BOWL | SUK KEUN KANG | 2017 | ZELKOVA WOOD, LACQUER

A natural lacquering process enhances the durability of these nesting bowls, carved from zelkova wood by Suk Keun Kang. Several coats of *ottchil* lacquer are applied and heat-cured, creating vessels that are safe for use with food, as well as resistant to water and heat, and even dishwasher-safe. *Ottchil* has been used since the Three Kingdoms period to protect everything from fine furniture to everyday utensils. Kang's method refines the tradition by replacing the long, climate-dependent drying process with heat-curing, producing faster and more consistent results while preserving the natural character of the wood.

옻칠 함지

JITAECHILGI | NAMGWON LYU | 2019 | HANJI, LACQUER

To create these storage boxes, Namgwon Lyu revived the traditional technique of *jitaechilgi*. This labour-intensive process involves coating sheets of *hanji* paper with *ottchil*, a lacquer derived from tree sap. The layers are built up to form a water-resistant surface, revealing the uneven textures of the paper's natural fibres.

지태칠기

BANJIKKORI | ANONYMOUS | JOSEON DYNASTY | PINE WOOD

The *banjikkori* is a traditional sewing box used to store needles, thread and small household tools. Essential to pre-modern domestic life, it was often part of a bride's dowry, symbolizing her readiness to manage a household. In homes where clothing was hand-sewn and frequently mended, such boxes were indispensable. This example, made of plain pine, lacks decoration but boasts an attractive decagonal design with two compartments.

반짇고리

CHEONGJA HAP | ANONYMOUS | GORYEO DYNASTY | CELADON

During the Goryeo Dynasty, small celadon (*cheongja*) lidded containers such as this one held incense, tea or cosmetic powders. This thirteenth-century example, probably from Gangjin or Buan, is defined by its low height and narrow diameter. It features a chrysanthemum motif, its petals in white and stem in black, set against the soft green glaze.

청자합

EAR PICK | ANONYMOUS | GORYEO DYNASTY | GOLD

This gold ear pick believed to date back to the early Goryeo Dynasty combines utility with ornament. One end tapers into a bamboo-like form for cleaning the ear canal, while the other bears a bell and butterfly motif. Measuring just a few centimetres long, it may also have functioned as a decorative hair accessory.

귀이개

TOBACCO BOXES | ANONYMOUS | JOSEON DYNASTY | IRON, SILVER

By the late Joseon period, smoking had become widespread and members of the elite commissioned ornate containers in which to keep their tobacco leaves. These boxes were embellished using the *eun ipsa* technique (see page 100). The example at top right has a snugly fitting lid incised with a large double-happiness character; the lid could be opened by pressing the button at the front. Another box, hexagonal in form, is patterned with the auspicious character *su* (long life), written in seal script. The same motif reappears on a rounded box, here accompanied by writhing dragons – symbols of cosmic power and protection.

담배함

CHAESANG | ANONYMOUS | BAMBOO

Chaesangjang is the craft of weaving bamboo baskets (*chaesang*) decorated with traditional Korean patterns using thinly cut and naturally dyed bamboo strips. The skill has been valued for centuries and is now on Korea's Intangible Cultural Heritage list. During the time of the Joseon Dynasty, *chaesang* were prized by women of the royal court and later became essential for storing clothes, accessories and other valuables. Although it is practised across the country, *chaesangjang* remains closely associated with Damyang in South Jeolla Province, which is known for its bamboo forests.

채
상

THE SOUND OF SPRING | SEONG IM JEON | 1995 | SEDGE

Wanggol is a tough sedge harvested from wetlands and riverbanks across Korea. Sun-dried and handwoven, it has long been valued for its resilience and breathability. For centuries, *wanggol* baskets were essential household items, particularly for storing food. Their airy weave kept grains, vegetables and dried fish from spoiling, while their light yet sturdy structure suited Korea's floor-sitting culture, where containers were required to be both portable and stackable. This contemporary example was crafted by Seong Im Jeon, director of the Pulzip Craft Museum (see also page 94).

봄소리

RELAXING
쉬
기

RELAXING

Traditionally, the Korean approach to rest was characterized by unhurriedness and intention. It centred on stillness and the freedom to move at one's own pace without constraint. This sensibility is encapsulated in the concept of *yeoyu*, which denotes composure, room to breathe and a life unburdened by haste. In contemporary Korea, however, such a lifestyle has become increasingly elusive. The prevailing culture of *ppalli-ppalli*, meaning 'faster, faster', reflects a society shaped by limited time and diminishing patience. In this context, *yeoyu* has become not only scarce but even aspirational.

Traditional Korean homes, or *hanok*, were designed in accordance with the ethos of *yeoyu*. Characterized by minimal furnishings and spatial clarity, *hanok* interiors were constructed around the concept of serenity. The low, horizontal orientation of these buildings, most with just a single story, fostered a sense of intimacy with the earth. In the winter, heating was provided by the *ondol* system, whereby warmth generated by the kitchen fire passed beneath the clay floors. To make the most of the heat, individuals would sit cross-legged on the floor, often using a *boryo*, a thick, quilted cushion (see page 117). In summer, these cushions would be swapped for versions made from such breathable materials as woven grass, *mosi* (ramie) or bamboo, selected for their cooling properties and textured surfaces that aid thermoregulation by wicking moisture from the skin.

The climatic extremes of the Korean summer – marked by humidity, still air and prolonged heat – have given rise to various design strategies intended to foster comfort and connection with one's natural surroundings. A *bal* (bamboo blind; see page 80) hung at the entrance of a home provides shade while permitting airflow and allowing soft light to permeate. As wind passes through the woven structure, it creates a soothing whispering sound. The *jukbuin* or 'bamboo wife' (see page 122) is another such invention: a cylindrical bolster woven from thin bamboo strips, cool to the touch and breathable. Embracing the *jukbuin* during sleep allows air to circulate around the body, offering relief during sultry nights.

Open-sided wooden pavilions known as *jeongja*, slightly elevated and integrated into the natural landscape (see page 132), also encourage connection with nature. These structures were designed not to dominate their surroundings but to exist harmoniously within them. During the Joseon Dynasty, *seonbi* (Confucian scholars) would frequent *jeongja* to read, write or compose poetry inspired by the natural world. These spaces were not silent, but open – inviting the layered sounds of wind, birds, water and far-off conversation to enter, overlap and be savoured as part of the experience of rest. *Jeongja* also serve as communal gathering places; often situated in village centres, among trees or on elevated ground, they offer shelter and a setting for social exchange.

True rest, in the Korean imagination, has always been rooted in nature. Everyday objects were traditionally crafted from such natural substances as clay, stone, wood and fibre, not only for practical or environmental reasons, but also from a belief in their capacity to promote health and harmony. Even in contemporary urban high-rise apartments, the desire to maintain contact with natural materials persists. *Dolchimdae*, or stone beds (see page 137), are one such example. Favoured particularly by members of the older generation, these beds are now typically heated by electric systems modelled on *ondol* technology, and are used without a mattress. Believed to enhance circulation, relieve joint and muscular pain, and help to release toxins from the body, *dolchimdae* represent a continuation of long-standing practices adapted to modern contexts.

In Korea, rest is not considered an act of withdrawal, but one of re-engagement – a return to the fundamental rhythms of the natural world. The pursuit of *yeoyu* continues in subtle forms: in the shifting patterns of sunlight behind a bamboo *bal*, in the tactile coolness of a *jukbuin*, in the quiet comfort of a *boryo*, and in the open stillness of a *jeongja*. Whether in solitude or with companionship, these moments embody a world view in which the natural and the human are not separate, but deeply interwoven.

GYEOP | YESL LEE | 2018 | BRASS, NOBANG (SHEER SILK)

겹

Gyeop (Layer), designed by Yesl Lee (see also pages 60 and 117), reimagines the traditional *byeongpung* (folding screen) for contemporary living. Drawing on the screen's historical role as both a spatial divider and a ceremonial object (see page 209), the design uses a slender frame to support two textiles – one sheer, one dense – layered to create partial transparency. This allows privacy while letting light, air and glimpses of the surrounding space flow through. *Gyeop* defines zones within a room while inviting quiet relaxation.

ANDONGPO JOGAKBO BOJAGI | DUKJOO CHOI | 2007 | HEMP

Dukjoo Choi grew up watching her grandmother sew together leftover scraps of fabric into *jogakbo*, a patchwork form of *bojagi* (wrapping cloth – see page 98). She didn't take up the practice herself until she was in her mid-forties, but she is now recognized for the precision and elegance of her geometric compositions. While many of her works are vibrant with natural dyes, this piece is hand-sewn from *andongpo* – a soft, translucent hemp cloth – in a subdued, neutral tone. Interested in the intersection of architecture and craft, Choi creates large-scale pieces that can be hung as screens or shades in order to soften the light in a space.

안동포 보자기

HANGING SPLIT NO. 247 | SOOYON KIM | 2024 | HEMP, RAMIE, STONE

The *Hanging Split* series is produced by Limn Seoul, a textile brand founded by designer Sooyon Kim. Each piece is constructed by stitching together panels of hemp and *mosi* (ramie). For the final touch, Kim – who regards stone as a vessel of stories and history – suspends small pebbles from the seams, adding structural weight but also imparting a sense of balance and vitality. In this way, the pieces can function simultaneously as shades, room dividers and decorative textiles.

발

BORYO BANGSEOK | YESL LEE | 2025 | COTTON, FABRIC

This cushion, created by Yesl Lee in collaboration with Onjium (see page 14), is inspired by the traditional *boryo*, a type of Korean floor cushion beloved for its firm-yet-soft texture and seasonal comfort – cool in summer, warm in winter. The design features a thick, cotton-filled base and a removable cover, secured with ties. The fabrics can be customized according to space, season, or personal taste, ranging from rare, quilted textiles to handwoven atelier fabrics and functional technical materials.

보료방석

WEDDING BEDDING SET | ANONYMOUS | COTTON, SILK, THREAD

혼수이불과베개

This brightly coloured quilt with matching pillows forms part of a bride's *honsu*, the dowry of bedding given at marriage to symbolize warmth, prosperity and harmony in the new household. Generally made from vivid silks or satins and stuffed with cotton, they were designed to balance comfort across the seasons. The covers were often embroidered with motifs and Chinese characters representing longevity and fortune, in such auspicious colours as red, green and yellow. Stored in a bedding chest, they were brought out for weddings, festivals and honoured guests – they were intended to endure for decades and to be passed down through generations.

BEGAETMO | ANONYMOUS | JOSEON DYNASTY | MOTHER-OF-PEARL

Rather than the soft pillows that are favoured today, people from the Goryeo to Joseon periods in Korea often rested their heads on *mokchim*, cylindrical or rectangular wooden headrests. These solid supports were believed to aid posture, circulation and restful sleep. The ends – *begaetmo* – were frequently decorated, as in this mother-of-pearl example with its striking tiger motif. Being the most visible part, the ends bore elaborate designs that served as both ornament and talismans, guarding against bad dreams and evil spirits. In aristocratic and royal households, such *begaetmo* were also displayed as luxury objects and treasured as heirlooms.

베갯모

CUSHION STOOL (CIRCLE BASE) | TEO YANG | 2023 | WALNUT VENEER, FABRIC

In Korean culture, offering a guest a cushion is a gesture of respect, hospitality and warmth. This stool by Eastern Edition – the furniture brand founded by acclaimed designer Teo Yang (see page 16) – playfully reinterprets that tradition, stacking two cushions atop a sculptural wooden base.

쿠션 스툴

LACQUERED CHAIRS | MINJAE KIM | 2018 | PINE WOOD, LACQUER

Among the earliest pieces in an ongoing series of sculptural wooden chairs by New York-based Minjae Kim, these models became part of a collection released by interiors brand Garcé Dimofski. Combining simplicity and playful expression, each chair is hand-carved from solid pine and finished with stain and lacquer.

락카 의자

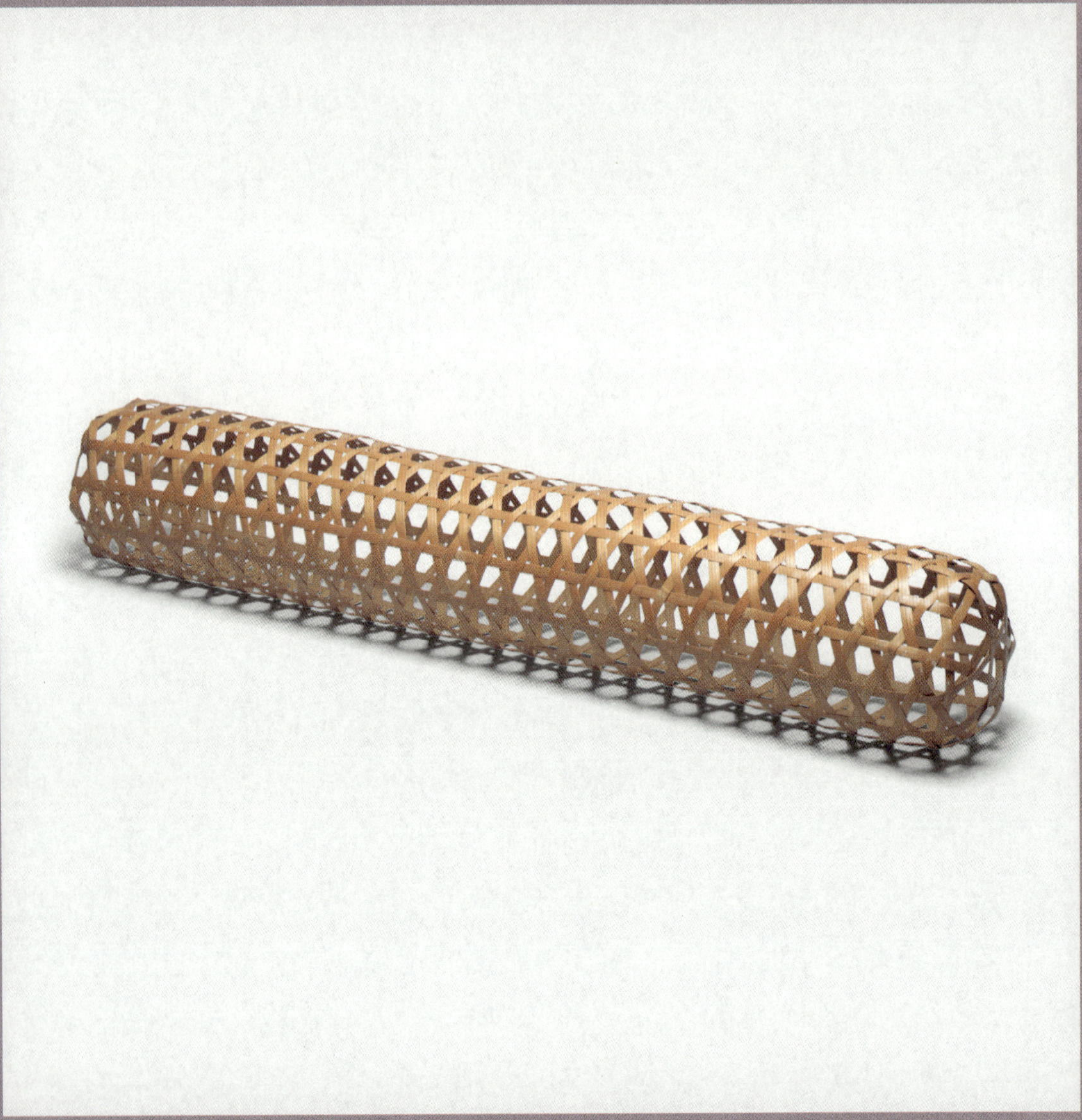

JUKBUIN | ANONYMOUS | BAMBOO

Jukbuin is a traditional Korean body pillow woven from split bamboo strips, designed to provide relief during hot summer nights. The name translates literally as 'bamboo wife', reflecting its role as a companion during sleep, when it would be embraced under a light hemp quilt. It is made by splitting and smoothing well-dried bamboo, then weaving the strips loosely into a hollow, cylindrical shape that allows air to circulate and keep the user cool. *Jukbuin* were traditionally crafted without nails or string.

죽부인

AMPLIFICATION OF SENSATION CHAIR | MAEZM | 2019 | RECYCLED PLASTIC

Evocative of a hand cupped around an ear, this chair's enveloping form is designed to amplify sound. Installed on the banks of Seoul's Han River – a rare urban refuge – the project by Maezm, a design studio run by Eun Whan Cho and Tai Ho Shin, enhances the ambient noise of flowing water and fosters a meditative connection with nature. Sustainability was a key concern in its creation, and each chair is carefully hand-cast in a large mould using a resin composite made from recycled plastic chips.

감각의 증폭

BLUE ARMCHAIR | KWANGHO LEE | 2022 | NYLON ROPE

Kwangho Lee began experimenting with knotted cord furniture for his graduation show at Hongik University in 2007. Since then, he has expanded the *Obsession* series to include an array of colourful pieces made from PVC tubing, nylon rope and electrical wire. Lee's inspiration comes from childhood memories of his grandfather's farm, where he learned to tie cords and witnessed furniture being fashioned from scrap materials and natural finds.

파란 안락의자

HYU CHAIR | WON DEOK KWON | 2023 | WALNUT WOOD, LEATHER

Carpenter Won Deok Kwon (see also page 91) is a specialist in *somok* – the traditional Korean woodworking technique that uses no nails or glue. He created this walnut chair as part of a bespoke set for the Youonejae Hot Spring Hotel in Chungbuk Province. Its legless form is designed specifically for floor-seated tea rituals, in keeping with long-standing Korean customs associated with hospitality and relaxation – *hyu* means 'rest' or 'pause'. 휴

TONE SIDE TABLES | SOHYUN YUN | 2019 | ACRYLIC

Part of Sohyun Yun's *Tone* series, these side tables draw inspiration from the colours of *hanbok*, Korea's traditional dress. Yun carefully selected harmonious hues and used them to hand-dye acrylic sheets. The dyed sheets were then formed into vibrant furnishings with pared-back, minimalist silhouettes.

톤 시리즈

PLAIN CUTS BOX CHAIR | WONMIN PARK | 2017 | ALUMINIUM

For his first solo exhibition – held at Carpenters Workshop Gallery in New York in 2015 – Wonmin Park departed from the resin works that had previously defined his practice. The *Plain Cuts* series presents a collection of minimalist furnishings with a cool, industrial sensibility. Constructed primarily from aluminium sheets with a mottled patina, the surfaces evoke the quiet imperfection of time-worn materials.

플레인컷 상자 의자.

SOFTEN | JINSIK KIM | 2020 | OAK WOOD

Seoul-based designer Jinsik Kim produced this oak coffee table in Lisbon in collaboration with Portuguese furniture brand Porventura. Inspired by the soft contours of marble sculpture, he shaped the piece with gently rounded, highly polished edges for a lightness that contrasts with its solid wood mass.

소프튼

W STOOL | KUNSIK CHOI | 2019 | ALUMINIUM, LACQUERED OAK WOOD

When Korean eyewear brand Projekt Produkt commissioned Kunsik Choi's studio (see also page 210) to design furniture for its flagship store in Seoul, he created a fourteen-piece collection that echoes the brand's sleek, high-tech aesthetic. While aluminium provides a clean, industrial edge, Choi softened the look with cylindrical silhouettes and tactile wooden surfaces, balancing precision with warmth.

더블유 스툴

SIDE TABLE | RAHEE YOON | 2024 | ACRYLIC

This side table by Rahee Yoon is crafted from opaque acrylic – a material she has explored in depth throughout her career. Drawn to its subtle luminosity and structural clarity, Yoon reimagines acrylic beyond its typical industrial use, treating it as a sculptural medium for collectible design. Her process involves precise hand-shaping and thermal bending, producing clean lines and soft silhouettes that give her pieces a quiet, architectural presence. This example was commissioned by Francis Gallery, which has spaces in Los Angeles, USA, and Bath, UK.

흰수평

BUCKWHEAT PILLOW | MOHM | 2017 | LINEN-COTTON BLEND, BUCKWHEAT

Founded in Buyeo – a town with deep craft traditions – Mohm is the studio of designers Sunjin Kim and Seoyoon Lim (see also page 160). These understated pillows are its modern take on traditional Korean neck pillows (see page 119). Filled with buckwheat hulls, they offer firm support and improved airflow, regulating heat and moisture for comfort during Korea's sweltering summers.

베개

JEONGJA | ANONYMOUS | WOOD, CEMENT, TILES

Jeongja are small, elevated timber pavilions with tiled roofs, often situated in gardens, by rivers or along scenic roadsides. In the Joseon period they served as places in which *seonbi* (Confucian scholars) could write, paint and engage in philosophical debate, the structures' open sides embodying the ideal of harmony with nature. They also functioned as communal rest stops for travellers and villagers, and many Koreans still use them as such today.

정
자

BUCHAE | ANONYMOUS | HANJI, BAMBOO

The *buchae* (fan) has long held both practical and cultural significance in Korea. It provided portable relief from the summer heat, while also serving as an aesthetic object, often painted, inscribed, and exchanged as a meaningful gift. This undecorated example, with its white *hanji* surface and plain bamboo ribs, reflects an aesthetic of purity and restraint, emphasising simplicity and natural form.

부채

BUDEUL BUCHAE | ANONYMOUS | JOSEON DYNASTY | BULRUSH, BAMBOO

This *budeul buchae* (bulrush fan) was known as *paldeokseon* – meaning 'fan with eight virtues' – owing to its multipurpose nature. In addition to keeping its owner cool, it supposedly had seven other functions, including shielding the user from light rain, repelling flies and mosquitoes, and acting as a seat. Early Korean fans were made from dried leaves or feathers, but the *paldeokseon* evolved into a flat, leaf-shaped fan woven from sedge or bulrush (*budeul*), fixed to a bamboo handle. Without ribs, its woven surface was strong yet flexible, making it suitable for its many uses.

부들부채

HAPJUKSEON | ANONYMOUS | JOSEON DYNASTY | HANJI, BAMBOO

The *hapjukseon* – literally 'joined bamboo fan' – is a traditional folding fan admired as much for its craft as for its utility. Slender strips of bamboo are split and joined to form the ribs, which are then covered with *hanji* paper. This example, composed of bamboo ribs and a surface of red *hanji*, features decorative characters symbolizing longevity (*su*) and geometric motifs painted on the guard sticks. Unlike rigid fans, the *hapjukseon* folds compactly and could be slipped into a sleeve or pocket, making it especially favoured by *seonbi* and members of the *yangban* elite.

합죽선

ADVERTISING FAN | ANONYMOUS | POST-LIBERATION | PAPER, BAMBOO, WOOD

광고 부채

After Korea's liberation in 1945, hand fans became a popular vehicle for advertising. Lightweight, inexpensive and indispensable in summer, they offered companies a visible and low-cost way of publicizing their products. This example, produced for Daeji Sewing Machine Company, promotes the 'Champion Sewing Machine'. With a wooden handle, bamboo ribs and paper cover, it bears the brand name and slogan, as well as a stylized illustration of a figure sheltering beneath an umbrella.

DOLCHIMDAE | ANONYMOUS | WOOD, STONE

The *dolchimdae* merges Korea's traditional *ondol* floor-heating system (for centuries Koreans slept directly on the heated floor) with the comfort of a Western-style bed. A thick stone slab – commonly granite, marble or jade – is set into a wooden frame and heated gently, either by electricity or by circulating water, retaining its warmth for hours. This design provides comfort during cold winters and is believed to improve circulation, ease joint stiffness and promote relaxation.

돌침대

ANSEOK | ANONYMOUS | HANJI, LACQUER, HAIR

안석

Ondol culture shaped Korean daily life. People ate, worked and rested on the floor, so furniture was minimal and cushions were essential for comfort. Unlike soft, padded cushions, *anseok* were firm, designed to provide back support when sitting for long periods. They were made from such materials as silk or ramie, but this example was created using the *jiseung* technique (see also page 58), whereby strips of *hanji* paper are twisted into cord, woven, and then lacquered for durability. The inside is stuffed with human hair.

LOW DESK (CHIM SERIES) | CHANHYEOK KIM | 2024 | COFFEE DOUGH, PAPER

Chanhyeok Kim explores the interplay between Korean tradition and modern design. Reinterpreting such familiar forms as the *soban* table (see pages 56 and 57) and simple wooden seating, he experiments with sculptural qualities and materials not generally associated with furniture, such as coffee dough and paper. This low desk is part of his CHim project (*chim* meaning both 'sink in' and 'depth'), the components of which are designed to integrate seamlessly with *hanok* interiors.

침

FLOW BENCH | JUNGJOO IM | 2024 | OAK WOOD, BRASS

Commissioned for a restaurant in Hawaii, the *Flow Bench* by Seoul-based designer Jungjoo Im takes its inspiration from the organic sway of tree branches. Hewn from a block of timber using a chainsaw, the form was then refined with a hand-planer to create its fluid, sweeping silhouette. Im's work with Korean timber is experimental and grounded in hand-shaped craft, drawing upon the traditional wood-turning technique known as *gal-e-jil*, a centuries-old Korean practice of carving rotating timber. 흐름

DAYBED | HYUNG SUK JO | 2012 | ASH WOOD, FABRIC

Seoul-based designer Hyung Suk Jo's *Daybed* reduces the Korean seating archetype to its essentials. Built from solid ash, it sits low and horizontal with a flat cushion and restrained armrest. The design draws on the understated beauty of Joseon-era furniture and traditional architecture, while also melding the efficiency of modern production with the subtle irregularity of hand-finished craft.

데이베드

WANGGOL HWABANGSEOK | SOLUNA LIVING | 2020 | SEDGE

The *wanggol hwabangseok* is a handwoven floor cushion made from dried sedge, traditionally used in *hanok*, where people would sit and work on the heated *ondol* floors. The sedge, known as *wanggol*, is harvested, sun-dried, braided and stitched with natural-fibre threads. Cool to the touch in the summer and insulating in the winter, these thin cushions were used in both daily life and ceremonial settings. This contemporary version is made by contemporary art and lifestyle brand Soluna Living using stems harvested from Ganghwa Island in northwestern Korea.

왕골 화방석

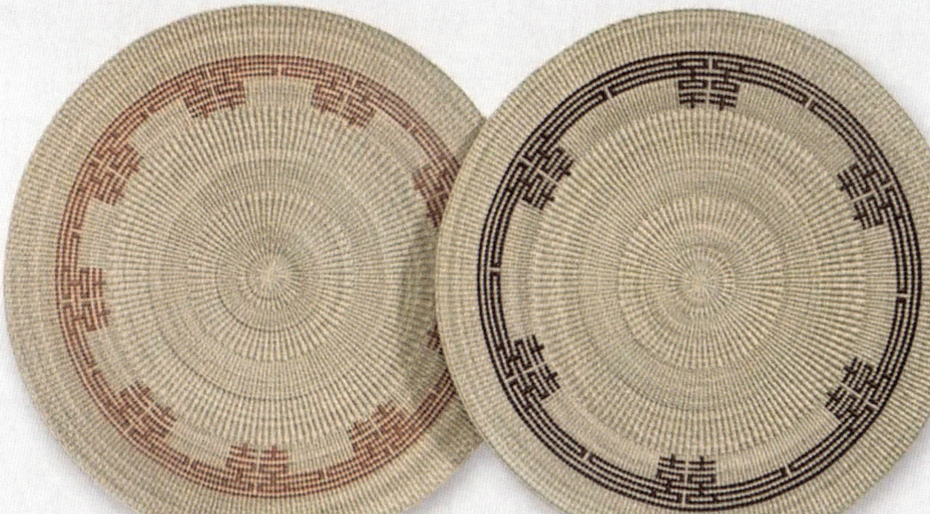

MARRIED COUPLE BANGSEOK | SUNG JA HUR | 2020 | RUSH

Handwoven by Sung Ja Hur, this version of the *bangseok* cushion is crafted from *wancho* (rush) grown in Korean wetlands. A material similar to *wanggol* (see opposite), its stems are slender and slightly softer than sedge, making it ideal for crafting mats and blinds. The woven motif features the *heeja* pattern, a stylized version of the Chinese character for 'joy', symbolizing harmony and good fortune.

부부방석

MODAM | ANONYMOUS | JOSEON DYNASTY | WOOL, COTTON

A *modam* is a Joseon-era carpet, typically woven from wool and cotton, that was used to bring warmth and beauty to the floor. In the eighteenth and nineteenth centuries, crane motifs such as this became especially fashionable, symbolizing longevity, nobility and auspicious fortune. Although few *modam* survive today – making them both rare and prized – they often appear in early Joseon portraits of officials and other elite figures.

모담

JARI MAT | SOLUNA LIVING | 2019 | SEDGE

This reimagining of *hwamunseok* – the woven sedge floor mat that has been part of Korean life for more than 1,300 years – is made using *wanggol* sedge cultivated on Ganghwa Island. Part of Soluna Living's *Jari* series, it retains the distinctive character of the traditional weave while highlighting the raw beauty of the material itself. Ganghwa sedge is shaped by the island's sea winds and renowned for its strength and durability, yielding mats of exceptional quality.

화문석

DRESSING

입기

DRESSING

Korea's textile and fashion traditions have evolved over centuries of war, colonization and industrialization. From the flowing, voluminous lines of *hanbok* (see page 161) and the breathability of such natural fibres as *sambae* and *mosi*, to contemporary designers reinterpreting historical forms and materials, Korean dress has long balanced aesthetic values with the practical needs of daily life. Comfort guided design: roomy trousers that allowed horse riding, and breathable hemp jackets that offered relief during the country's humid summers.

The *hanbok* lies at the heart of traditional Korean dress. Shaped by the country's nomadic past, where horse riding was central to daily life and mobility and functionality were essential, garments were designed with ease of movement in mind. Women's *hanbok* typically consisted of two main pieces: the *jeogori*, a cropped long-sleeved top; and the *chima*, a high-waisted, full skirt. Men wore wide-legged trousers paired with a long overcoat. Both silhouettes offered freedom of motion as well as graceful lines. Variations in cut and material reflected social status; royalty wore richly dyed silks, while commoners dressed in unbleached cotton or hemp. In the summer, unlined garments were made of *mosi*, a fine ramie, or *sambae*, a coarse hemp, both of which allowed the body to breathe. In the winter, quilted *nubi* garments provided insulation.

All these garments were strongly informed by the natural fibres found across the peninsula. Among the most important were *mosi*, *sambae* and *myeongju* (silk), each prized not only for its practical qualities, but also for its cultural significance. *Mosi*, long regarded as the ideal summer fabric, is light, breathable and translucent. Its production involves a slow, painstaking process by which ramie plants are stripped, softened, spun and handwoven into cloth. The resulting fabric is cool to the touch, with a delicate sheen.

By contrast, *sambae* was the fabric of the everyday. Coarser and more robust, it was traditionally favoured by the working classes for its durability, moisture resistance and affordability. The material embodies a kind of honest beauty aligned with Korea's long-standing respect for simplicity and utility. *Sambae* was also commonly used in funeral attire, its plainness thought to reflect humility, and its affordability ensuring access regardless of status.

The lustrous silk *myeongju*, meanwhile, was reserved for the upper classes. Unlike the airy transparency of *mosi*, *myeongju* offers a soft, luxurious drape and can be dyed in rich hues, making it ideal for traditional embroidery and ceremonial dress. It was worn by *seonbi* scholars, aristocrats and royalty for weddings, rituals and ancestral rites, its elegance reinforcing its place in symbolic and official contexts.

These textiles were never merely practical. They embody a wider Korean aesthetic: modest, refined and deeply attuned to nature. The breathability of these garments speaks to a cultural ideal of a harmonious relationship between body, clothing and the natural world.

One of the most evocative expressions of this ideal lies in traditional wedding attire. Bridal garments were layered and ornate; the *hwarot* (see page 165) or *wonsam* (see page 168), long ceremonial coats worn over the *hanbok*, were richly embroidered with phoenixes, peonies and butterflies, motifs that symbolized virtue, prosperity and fertility. The outfit was completed with a *jokduri*, a decorative headpiece. The bride's face was also marked with *yeonji gonji* – crimson dots painted on the cheeks and forehead to ward off evil spirits. The groom's attire was more understated, consisting of a simple robe and the black *gat* (see page 151), a horsehair hat symbolizing scholarly dignity and maturity. Together, these garments were rich in symbolism, enacting marriage as a sacred transition shaped by tradition, harmony and respect.

Footwear, too, held meaning. *Gomusin* (see page 180) – rubber shoes introduced in the early twentieth century – were inexpensive and mass-produced. They echoed the form of traditional shoes but were cast entirely in black or white rubber. Worn by students, housewives and workers, they came to symbolize Korea in transition: enduring hardship, yet moving forwards. By contrast, *kkotsin* (see page 172), silk shoes embroidered with floral motifs, were reserved for ceremonial wear by women and children. Worn for weddings, birthdays or holidays, they embodied joy, beauty and good fortune. Together, *gomusin* and *kkotsin* reflect the dual nature of Korean material culture: practical and poetic, modern and traditional.

More recently, Korean design has continued to reflect the realities of everyday life with quiet ingenuity. One modest yet effective example is the *eongdeongi uija* (literally, 'buttocks chair', see page 181) – a low, portable seat with a strap designed to be worn around the waist to support a lifestyle centred on squatting and floor-sitting. Still commonly used by elderly farmers, it helps to reduce strain from repeated sitting and standing during planting and harvesting. Although modern machinery has reshaped rural labour, the 'buttocks chair' endures as a cherished object, a symbol of care for the ageing body and of respect for manual work.

With Korea's rapid modernization came a shift towards Western clothing. Today, *hanbok* is mostly reserved for special occasions – national holidays, weddings and ancestral rites. Yet the legacy of traditional materials endures. Such fabrics as *mosi* and *sambae* have found new life in bedding, cushions and garments designed for contemporary interiors. Valued for their breathability and quick-drying qualities, they resonate with a growing interest in sustainable, heritage-based design. This turn reflects Korea's capacity for adaptation, not simply preserving traditional wisdom, but reimagining it to meet the needs of modern life.

Korean material culture continues to evolve, not only through aesthetics, but also through quiet, deeply functional responses to the everyday. In Korea, clothing is more than adornment; it is a language of comfort, care and continuity.

JEONGJAGWAN | KYUNG HEE KIM | 2016 | HORSEHAIR

The *jeongjagwan* was a traditional indoor hat worn by *sadaebu*, members of the educated aristocracy during the Joseon period, who were typically Confucian scholars, government officials and community leaders. At the time, upper-class men were expected to keep their heads covered at all times. Made from woven horsehair, the hat had multiple peaks that evoked mountains and constituted symbols of honour and wisdom, reinforcing the noble status of the wearer. This award-winning contemporary example was crafted by Kyung Hee Kim.

정자관

GAT | ANONYMOUS | JOSEON DYNASTY | HORSEHAIR, BAMBOO

The Korean *gat* was a cylindrical hat with a wide brim, primarily worn by the *yangban* elite while outdoors or performing ceremonies during the Joseon Dynasty. Made chiefly from bamboo and horsehair over a bamboo frame, its semi-transparent black weave subtly revealed the wearer's face. The top was finished with *hanji* paper, then painted with ink and lacquer. High-ranking men would adorn theirs with gold, silver, amber and jade.

갓

SATGAT | ANONYMOUS | JOSEON DYNASTY | BAMBOO

The *satgat* was a conical bamboo hat designed to offer protection from sun and rain. Its broad brim could also obscure the wearer's eyes, lending anonymity. It was traditionally worn by farmers and travellers, as well as Buddhist monks. Unlike most Joseon-era headgear, which marked social rank, the *satgat* was purely functional – a rural parallel to the umbrella of today.

삿
갓

SANGMO | ANONYMOUS | JOSEON DYNASTY | RICE STRAW, PAPER

Made from rice straw and topped with paper streamers, this hat, of a type known as *sangmo*, was worn during Korean folk performances. It was particularly popular for *pungmul*, a tradition combining drumming, dancing and singing. As the performer danced and whipped their head around, the tassels spun in wide arcs, amplifying the dynamism of the movements and captivating the audience with their rhythmic, celebratory motion.

상모

GULGEON | ANONYMOUS | JOSEON DYNASTY | RAMIE, STRAW

Gulgeon was a traditional head covering worn by the chief mourner (commonly a male relative, such as a son or grandson) in Joseon-era funeral rites. Made of stiffened cloth, it featured a three-fold pleated design and was typically worn with *sangbok* (traditional hemp mourning clothes) over an inner cloth cap. Sometimes it was secured with a straw forehead band known as *sujil*. The exact length of mourning varied by relationship, with parents warranting longer terms – sometimes two years or more.

굴건

GATJIP | ANONYMOUS | JOSEON DYNASTY | HANJI

This *gatjip* (*gat* case) was designed to protect the delicate bamboo-and-horsehair *gat* (see page 151) of the Joseon *yangban* elite. Crafted from several layers of durable *hanji* paper, it features an accordion fold for ease of access. The top is decorated with the *taegeuk* (or *taiji*) motif – the yin-yang symbol representing cosmic balance – that is also found on the contemporary Korean flag.

갓
집

HAHOETAL | ANONYMOUS | JOSEON DYNASTY | WOOD

Hahoetal are wooden masks used in the Hahoe Byeolsingut Talnori, a masked dance-drama originating in Hahoe Village in Andong, North Gyeongsang Province. The performance blends ritual, satire and entertainment, dating back to the Goryeo Dynasty. Carved with exaggerated expressions, the masks fall into three main types – female, male and animal – each embodying social roles, humour and folklore. Today, the making of *Hahoetal* remains an iconic Korean folk craft, celebrated for its artistry, expressive power and enduring connection to tradition and communal memory.

하회탈

NORIGAE | CHRISTINA KIM | 2023 | FABRIC, THREAD

Norigae is a traditional ornamental pendant worn with *hanbok*, suspended either from the ties of the *jeogori* (jacket) or from the *chima* (skirt) waist. They are thought to have evolved from *yopae*, waist ornaments worn in the Silla Kingdom during the Three Kingdoms period. Designs varied in shape, colour and material, from precious metals to silk tassels. These contemporary designs by Christina Kim were made by hand using leftover scraps of fabric, and symbolize protection from misfortune.

노리개

NORIGAE | DAHYE JEONG | 2017 | HORSEHAIR, WOODEN BEADS, THREAD

Seoul-based artisan Dahye Jeong (see also pages 97 and 200) reimagines the *norigae* using the ancient craft of horsehair weaving, encasing strands in intricate knots around a string of wooden beads. Jeong begins her process by carefully selecting suitable horsehair, looking for strands that are even in thickness, smooth, lustrous and durable. With a needle, she then weaves the fibres across a wooden frame that she has carved into the desired form. The weave must remain taut, and the wood beneath ensures the strands stay firmly in place.

노리개

JIPSIN | ANONYMOUS | RICE STRAW

Jipsin are the archetypal Korean sandals woven from straw, and have been worn since ancient times. Typically made from leftover rice straw after harvest, they were simple to make and most households made their own. They were prone to damage, however, so travellers would often carry several pairs for long journeys. Common until the early twentieth century, they were gradually replaced by rubber *gomusin* (see page 180).

짚신

BEOSEON | MOHM | 2017 | LINEN-COTTON BLEND

Mohm (see also page 131) was established in Buyeo, a small town renowned for its rich crafting heritage. The studio, founded by designers Sunjin Kim and Seoyoon Lim, works with local artisans to craft its minimalist collections. These slippers, inspired by *beoseon* (traditional Korean socks, see page 175), were designed in 2017 as part of their first ever collection, *SoBaek*.

버
선

FROST | CHRISTINA KIM | 2023 | SILK

서리

Artist and designer Christina Kim (see also page 157) reinterprets traditional textiles through a contemporary lens, bridging craft and design while honouring and repurposing heritage practices. Drawing on the flowing lines of the *hanbok*, she reimagines them through layering and transforming undergarments into outerwear. *Frost* takes inspiration from the icy stillness of winter mornings, through fabrics in twenty subtle shades of white. The work emerged from a collaboration with Onjium Clothing Studio, the research and artisan branch of the Arumjigi Foundation (see page 14).

JANGOT | ANONYMOUS | JOSEON DYNASTY | SILK

The *jangot* was a long overcoat worn by women of the Joseon era, which could be draped over the head to conceal the face in public. While it also offered protection from the sun and dust, its primary role reflected Confucian values of modesty and propriety, which required women to veil themselves outside the home. Usually made of fine silk, the *jangot* was most often worn by women of the *yangban* elite class, who could afford such garments. The green sheen and flowing form of this example embody both elegance and restraint, encapsulating the social codes of its time.

장옷

KING YEONGJO'S DOPO | KYUNG SUN LEE | 2017 | SILK

The *dopo* was the defining robe of the late Joseon era, worn by kings, officials and *seonbi* scholars. Originating in the sixteenth century as a Korean adaptation of the Chinese *daopao*, it developed a distinct form: a straight collar forming a V-neck, long rectangular body panels and wide attached sleeves. Materials varied with the season; ramie or hemp were worn in the summer, and silk or cotton in the winter. This reproduction of King Yeongjo's *dopo*, dating from 1740, is made from plain-woven silk gauze dyed pale green, with a ramie collar. It was reproduced in 2017 by Kyung Sun Lee of Onjium Clothing Studio (see also page 166) for an exhibition by Arumjigi.

영조 도포

BOKJUMEONI | ANONYMOUS | SILK

The *bokjumeoni* is a small silk pouch traditionally worn with *hanbok*, usually concealed beneath the jacket. Embroidered with auspicious motifs or the Chinese character *bok*, meaning blessing or good fortune, it symbolizes prosperity and protection. A decorative knot secures the pouch; more than a fastening, this is part of Korea's knotting tradition, *maedeup*, and is believed to 'trap' good luck. Although practical as a storage item, the *bokjumeoni* also served as a keepsake imbued with blessings, and many were treasured long after the festive occasion for which they were made.

복주머니

HWAROT | ANONYMOUS | JOSEON DYNASTY | SILK, THREAD

Once reserved for royalty, the *hwarot* (woman's ceremonial robe) became fashionable among the upper classes in the late Joseon period. It was made from silk and typically adorned with auspicious motifs, such as peonies, lotuses, butterflies and phoenixes, representing wealth, vitality and marital harmony. This example displays vivid reds and golds, with peaches and pomegranates embroidered on the shoulders to signify longevity and fertility. Given their value, these robes were often handed down through generations – the white cuffs could be replaced to keep the garment looking fresh.

활옷

GUUI | KYUNG SUN LEE | 2021 | LEATHER

The *guui*, also known as *gatot*, was a distinctive overcoat of the Joseon Dynasty, made from leather and worn for warmth during Korea's harsh winters. Its broad sleeves and straight silhouette allowed easy layering, while the stitched leather provided durability and insulation. Because leather was rarer and costlier than woven cloth, such garments were uncommon and typically worn by those of higher rank, or for travel and outdoor activities requiring extra protection. This contemporary replica, crafted by Kyung Sun Lee of Onjium Clothing Studio (see also page 163), is based on an original deer-skin garment worn by General Nam Iheung at the end of the sixteenth century.

구의

NUBI JEOGORI | ANONYMOUS | COTTON, WOOL PADDING

Nubi, meaning 'to stitch together', is a traditional Korean quilting technique whereby two or more layers of fabric are sewn together, often with cotton or wool padding sandwiched within, to create a softly padded textile. Primarily employed to make jackets, trousers and duvets, it was a necessary response to Korea's harsh winters, since the stitched layers trap air, providing excellent insulation.

누빔 저고리

WONSAM | ANONYMOUS | 1935 | SILK

The *wonsam* is a traditional formal robe worn by women during significant occasions, such as weddings and ancestral rites. Characterized by a long, flowing silhouette and vibrant colours, it was typically crafted from fine silk. Unlike the richly embroidered *hwarot* (see page 165), which was adorned with auspicious motifs, the *wonsam* conveyed hierarchy and dignity through colour and form rather than decoration. This particular example was worn by Seon Hui Kim for her wedding to poet Gwang Gyun Kim in 1935.

원삼

MALGUN | EUN MI JEONG | 2019 | SILK

The *malgun* was a voluminous over-garment worn in Joseon Korea mainly by royal and upper-class women for horseback riding, although genre paintings also depict men layering it over long robes (*po*). Pulled on over the skirt, it featured wide legs open at the back and hem, gathered high at the chest and fastened at the ankles to secure the layers beneath – its swelling volume amplified the idealized silhouette of women's *hanbok*. The garment remained in courtly use until the early nineteenth century, before fading from daily life as women rode less. This is a contemporary copy of *malgun* excavated from a tomb, made using silk dyed with natural pigments.

말군

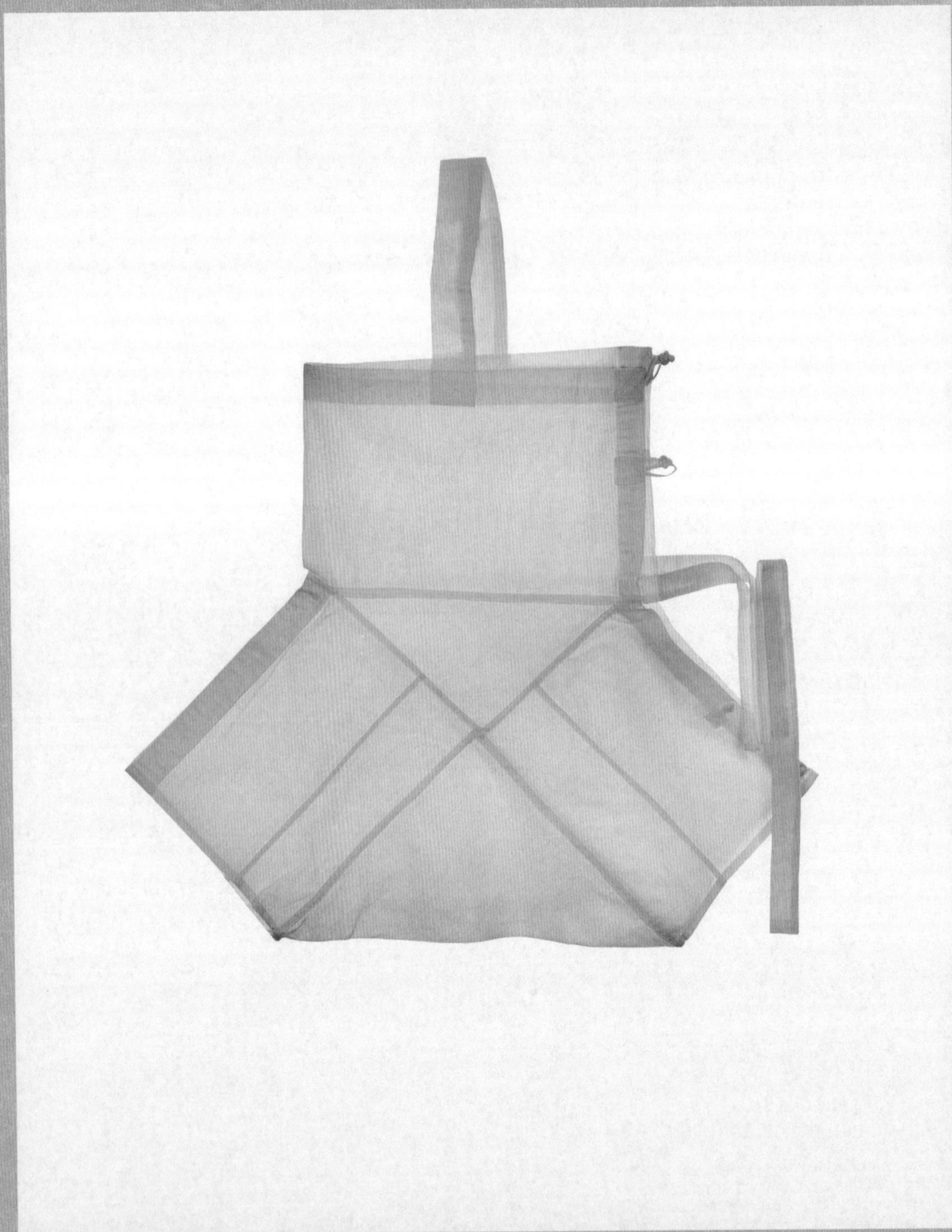

MUL OT | ANONYMOUS | LINEN

Mul ot (water clothing) was the work attire of Jeju Island's *haenyeo*, female divers who harvested abalone, seaweed and shellfish from the sea. Fastened by a strap over one shoulder, it stayed secure without constricting the chest or waist, allowing ease of movement underwater. It was cut for agility and made from lightweight linen that dries quickly, preventing the fabric from becoming heavy. The *mul ot* embodies the resourcefulness and endurance of the *haenyeo*, whose centuries-old traditions continue to this day.

물옷

SALCHANG GOJAENGI | ANONYMOUS | JOSEON DYNASTY | RAMIE

Gojaengi were a type of undergarment worn beneath women's skirts (*chima*), particularly suited to Korea's hot summers. This variant, called *salchang gojaengi*, was common in the Andong, Bonghwa and Yeongju regions of North Gyeongsang Province. Its distinctive feature was the small incisions (*salchang*) cut into the waistband with scissors, allowing air to circulate freely. Woven from *mosi* (ramie), the garment was especially light and cooling, bringing comfort during the humid summer months.

살창고쟁이

KKOTSIN | HAN GAP HWANG | JOSEON DYNASTY | SILK, HANJI, LEATHER

꽃신

The finely crafted silk shoes known as *kkotsin* – literally 'flower shoes' – would have been worn by women with the traditional brightly coloured *hanbok*. Dyed a vivid red and embroidered with floral and butterfly motifs, this particular pair was made by Han Gap Hwang, the last shoemaking master of the Joseon Dynasty, who also crafted the red shoes worn by the late nineteenth-century Emperor Gojong on special occasions. The lining is made from *hanji*, while the outsole is finished in leather. *Kkotsin* are a designated part of Korea's national cultural heritage.

GULLE | ANONYMOUS | JOSEON DYNASTY | SILK, THREAD

A *gulle* is a form of traditional headpiece (*sseugae*) from the late Joseon period, worn primarily by young girls from upper-class families, especially on their first birthday. Designed to ward off evil spirits, these hats featured interwoven silk bands hanging below the chin and were often embroidered with symbols of good fortune and longevity, such as tigers and peonies.

굴레

DURU DURU JUMEONI | YOUNG EUN KIM | 2021 | SILK, JADE BEADS

After graduating from the Design Academy Eindhoven, Young Eun Kim returned to Korea with a renewed desire to engage with the country's craft heritage. She began studying *chimseon*, the meticulous needlework techniques used to make *hanbok*. During the Joseon Dynasty, garments typically lacked pockets, so people carried their belongings in small pouches known as *durujumeoni*. Still used in ceremonies today – children receive them filled with money at Lunar New Year – these pouches symbolize good fortune. Kim's contemporary version is made from silk and finished with delicate jade beads.

두루두루 주머니

BEOSEON | ANONYMOUS | FABRIC, SILK

Beoseon are traditional socks typically worn with *hanbok*. Shaped to fit the foot, and typically made of white cotton (silk being reserved for royalty), they balanced warmth, protection, practicality and elegance. They originated in the Three Kingdoms period, when simple cloth wrappings evolved into the curved foot shape we know today. By the late nineteenth century, modern socks had largely replaced *beoseon*, which are now generally worn only during weddings and national celebrations.

버선

BINYEO | ANONYMOUS | JOSEON DYNASTY | JADE

Traditional Korean hairpins, known as *binyeo*, were used by women both to secure a chignon and as ornamental accessories. This particular example is made from jade, although *binyeo* could also be crafted from gold or other precious materials, and were often lavishly designed. Such pins also served as markers of marital status, being first worn during a woman's coming-of-age ceremony, signalling her transition into adulthood. During the Joseon Dynasty, hairpins adorned with plum blossom or bamboo motifs were especially popular, symbolizing fidelity in accordance with prevailing Confucian virtues.

비녀

FINE-TOOTHED COMB | ANONYMOUS | JOSEON DYNASTY | BAMBOO

Typically made from bamboo, these fine-toothed combs were used to smooth already combed hair and to apply oil for sheen. In a Confucian society in which the body was seen as a gift from one's parents, every strand of hair was to be treated with care. The comb thus embodied both grooming and filial piety. This example bears the Chinese characters for longevity and fortune, as well as its provenance.

참빗

HYUNGBAE | ANONYMOUS | JOSEON DYNASTY | SILK, THREAD

The *hyungbae* was an embroidered silk patch worn on the front and back of official robes to denote rank within the Joseon court. Introduced by the Ming Dynasty in China, the badges served as a form of insignia, with specific motifs signifying particular offices: cranes (such as this one) for civil officials; tigers or leopards for military officials; and dragons for kings and crown princes. Queen consorts and crown princesses wore *hanbok* adorned with the mythical bird *fenghuang*.

흉배

SANGTUGWAN | ANONYMOUS | JOSEON DYNASTY | LEATHER, WOOD

The *sangtu* was a topknot hairstyle traditionally worn by Korean men upon marriage or entry into adulthood. Long hair was left unbraided, brushed upwards and tied high on the head, secured with a hairpin known as *sangtugwan*. Crafted from a variety of materials, including wood, bamboo, leather and ox horn, the pin held the knot in place and helped to conceal it, as during the Joseon Dynasty it was considered impolite to expose the *sangtu*. The topknot hairstyle remained in use until late nineteenth-century reforms mandated short hair as part of state-led modernization.

상투관

GOMUSIN | ANONYMOUS | RUBBER

Gomusin are traditional Korean shoes made from rubber, introduced in the early twentieth century with the rise of mass production in factories. The men's style was modelled on the traditional leather shoes known as *gatsin*, and the women's on *danghye*, which were often made of silk and embroidered. More practical than their predecessors, they were wider, low-heeled, waterproof and durable, and their ease of maintenance made them popular among people of all classes. The first recorded wearer was Sunjong, the last emperor of Korea, in the opening decade of the twentieth century.

고무신

EONGDEONGI UIJA | ANONYMOUS | PLASTIC, FOAM, TEXTILES

Many traditional Korean daily activities – such as gardening, washing vegetables, sorting grains or selling produce at market – were carried out close to the ground, often in a low squat. From the late twentieth century onwards, portable *eongdeongi uija* (literally 'buttocks chair') began to appear, usually made of plastic and foam. Lightweight, inexpensive and durable, they quickly became a staple, especially in rural households. Their low, supportive form allows the body to rest while keeping the knees bent, easing strain on legs and back.

엉덩이 의자

RITUAL, PLAYING & DECORATING

의례와 놀이 및 꾸미기

RITUAL, PLAYING & DECORATING

In agrarian societies where life depended on the soil and weather, folk beliefs emerged as a way to navigate nature's unpredictability and to strengthen communal bonds. Over time, these beliefs became woven into daily life, passed down in forms shaped by Korean values and temperament. They laid the foundation for traditional practices, from such games as *yutnori* (see page 213) to ancestral rites like *jesa*, where offerings and prayers were made for health, prosperity and favourable weather.

The earliest forms of *jesa* date back to a time when shamanistic beliefs prevailed. People believed that ancestral and natural spirits influenced such events as rain, harvests and illness. To maintain harmony and earn protection, communities offered food and performed rituals – bowing, praying and making gestures of reverence. With the rise of the Joseon Dynasty, Confucianism became the guiding ideology, and *jesa* evolved into an expression of filial piety: *hyo*. These family-centred ceremonies were held on the anniversary of an ancestor's death or at seasonal transitions, offering a means of honouring and expressing gratitude to one's forebears. The *jesasang* (see page 208) – the ritual table – differed slightly between households but was always arranged with great care so as to place seasonal foods and fruit in symbolic positions. More than a meal, it was a way of communing with the dead.

A key object in the *jesa* ritual was the *byeongpung* (see page 209), a folding screen set behind the *jesasang* and often painted with landscapes, birds, flowers or calligraphy. In the open layout of a *hanok*, it served as both a backdrop and a spatial boundary, framing the ritual and heightening its significance.

One of Korea's oldest traditional games, *yutnori*, was played using four carved wooden sticks. Although enjoyed for its entertainment, it was also tied to seasonal rites and agricultural festivals, especially Seollal (Lunar New Year). In a society where the year's harvest depended on nature's favour, playing *yutnori* was believed to bring good luck and ensure abundance, and entire villages often joined in. It was a communal act of hope, a ritualized way of seeking control over the uncontrollable, where play and spiritual practice became one.

As communities modernized, new forms of play emerged. Among them was *gonggi* (see page 214), a simple game similar to jacks, played with five small pebbles or, more recently, plastic stones. Widely popular in schools from the early twentieth century onwards, it probably originated in rural villages, where children passed the time with whatever was close at hand.

While many traditional Korean objects served practical or ritual functions, a parallel tradition of decorative craft also flourished, producing pieces that were created simply to be admired, discussed or contemplated. Among the most iconic is the *dalhangari*, or moon jar (see page 186), developed during the Joseon Dynasty, when modesty and purity were prized ideals. These large, rounded porcelain vessels often bear subtle irregularities, perhaps an uneven rim, or a faint seam where the two halves were joined. Rather than flaws, such characteristics were seen as expressions of a Confucian sensibility: true beauty lies in the unforced, the humble and the incomplete. Although most were created purely for aesthetic appreciation, moon jars embodied a deeper harmony: between people and nature, imperfection and virtue.

From ancestral prayers to the flick of a hand in play, from ritual tables to porcelain jars, Korean agrarian life nurtured a culture in which the sacred and the playful, the functional and the symbolic, existed in quiet, meaningful balance.

MOON JAR | ANONYMOUS | JOSEON DYNASTY | WHITE PORCELAIN

The term moon jar (*dalhangari*) is a modern designation, inspired by the vessel's generous, rounded form and milky-white glaze. First appearing in the late seventeenth century, these large porcelain jars were made by joining two thrown hemispheres, often resulting in subtle asymmetry as they slumped or warped slightly in the kiln. Such irregularities were not corrected but embraced, reflecting the period's appreciation for natural imperfection. Although moon jars were sometimes used for storage, they regularly served ceremonial roles. They were displayed in royal palaces during diplomatic visits, their restrained form an expression of ideal Confucian taste.

백자 달항아리

MOON JAR | DONG JUN KIM | 2017 | WHITE PORCELAIN

In the twenty-first century a new generation of Korean designers has revived the form of the moon jar, often adding their own contemporary touch. Dong Jun Kim, however, has earned distinction by adhering to the traditional proportions and time-honoured techniques. He fires his porcelain jars in a wood-fired kiln for seventeen hours, a method that introduces subtle irregularities to the opaline surface. His studio is based in Mungyeong, a region with a long-standing ceramic heritage. Once home to royal kilns during the Joseon Dynasty, Mungyeong has for centuries been a centre of Korean pottery, known for its high-quality clay and skilled artisans.

달항아리

CHEONGJA MINI VASE | JINHO CHOI | 2023 | PORCELAIN

Celadon ceramics – known as *cheongja* – have been celebrated for more than a thousand years for their soft jade-green glaze and exquisite craft. Once reserved for temples, palaces and aristocratic homes, these pieces remain emblems of Korean artistic heritage. Yeongwol-based ceramicist Jinho Choi reinterprets the form in a subtle light-blue glaze, reimagining celadon for the contemporary domestic space.

청자 단아 화병

POLYGONAL CONTAINER | SEO HEE PARK | 2019 | PORCELAIN

Seo Hee Park draws on the legacy of *cheongja*, throwing each vessel on a wheel and finishing it by hand before glazing it in the signature jade-like hue. Internationally exhibited and now held in the permanent collection of the Victoria & Albert Museum in London, Park's work extends celadon beyond its historical ceremonial context, positioning it as a medium of modern expression that is at once restrained and quietly radical.

INCENSE BURNER | ANONYMOUS | GORYEO DYNASTY | CELADON

Made during the twelfth century, when Goryeo celadon reached its peak, this incense burner features a main chamber, in which the incense was placed, and a lion-shaped lid. Smoke and scent escape through the lion's gaping mouth, bringing the piece to life. Its pale blue-green glaze carries a soft sheen, and its form reflects the era's fascination with auspicious animals.

향로

ORIENTAL MOON | HYEJEONG KIM | 2019 | STONEWARE

Born in Japan to Korean parents, Hyejeong Kim creates works that exist between sculpture and utility. The Oriental Moon pot is part of her *Carpel* series of vessels, which are thrown on the wheel and then altered by hand. Rippling textures interrupt the smooth turquoise-glazed surface, evoking the natural imperfections of human skin or matured fruit.

동양의 달

EXPANDED FRAGMENTS NO. 2 | MINYEOL CHO | 2024 | DENIM, GLUE

Minyeol Cho's series *Expanded Fragments* is made from discarded denim remnants sourced from Seoul's garment district. He constructs each vessel by cutting and stacking the fabric scraps, gradually adjusting the level of bleach applied to the material to produce a soft ombré effect. Once the form is complete, it is sealed with natural glue to maintain its structure.

증축된 조각들

FLOW | JUNSU KIM | 2024 | VEGETABLE TANNED LEATHER

Having trained in metalwork and jewellery at Seoul's Kookmin University, Junsu Kim turned to leather after working with artisans in Tuscany. His fascination with the material led to a series of sculptural bowls, created by coiling strips of vegetable-tanned leather of varying lengths and widths. The resulting forms are finished with *ottchil* (a traditional Korean lacquer made from the refined sap of the *ott* tree), producing a durable and richly glossy surface.

흐름

INBORN OTT-003 | SUNG YOUL PARK | 2019 | LACQUER

Sung Youl Park reimagines the ancient Korean lacquer tradition of *ottchil* by using the sap-based resin not as a surface finish, but as a structural material. He applies layers of lacquer on to a mould to create a free-standing form, which he then decorates with fine strands of coloured *ott*, producing a richly textured, tactile finish.

본연

PRUNING | MINWOOK KIM | 2023 | ZELKOVA WOOD

A self-taught woodturner based in Busan, Minwook Kim centres his practice on a reverence for wood's natural life cycle. He embraces the material's weathered textures, rings and even signs of woodworm as part of its ongoing story. He shapes each piece meticulously on a lathe before allowing the wood to dry and settle naturally, creating works that change over time.

TRANSITION_IRREGULAR RHYTHM | JAIIK LEE | 2021 | COPPER, GOLD LEAF

In his *Transition* series, Jaiik Lee takes the concept of the moon jar (see page 186) and reimagines it in an entirely different material. Rather than using clay, Lee casts the forms in metal, applying ceramic pigments and finishing each piece with gold leaf. His jars depart from the symmetry of their historic counterparts, adopting fluid, organic silhouettes that gently distort tradition.

트랜지션 부정리듬

TRANSITION OF TRACES | SUNGHO CHO | 2019 | SILVER

Silversmith Sungho Cho's paper-thin silver vessels are formed through roll-printing and stamping techniques that leave subtle traces on the surface. Inspired by textures found in clothing, architecture and nature, Cho sometimes incorporates impressions taken from wax rubbings made at historical sites – such as a 600-year-old stone bridge in Seoul, and the Berlin Wall.

흔적의 전이

COURTYARD VASE | STUDIO MILLIONROSES | 2024 | COLOURED GLASS

Studio Millionroses, based in Seoul, is a collaboration between designer Hyung Moon Choi and photographer Joo Young Kim. Their Courtyard vase is made from coloured glass panels set on a sturdy aluminium base. Angular panels of varying heights form an architectural silhouette, evoking the layered courtyards of traditional Korean homes.

코트야드

DAAM DAH PLATE | KEE RYONG CHOI | 2022 | GLASS, GOLD LEAF

For his *Daam Dah* series, Scotland-based glass artist Kee Ryong Choi introduced tiny air bubbles into the glass – imperfections that are usually avoided in glassmaking. Rather than concealing them, he emphasized these irregularities by adorning them with flecks of gold foil. The technique draws on *sanggam*, an inlay method used for centuries by Korean artisans to embed patterns and motifs into ceramic and glass surfaces.

담다

GAREUM | DAHYE JEONG | 2024 | HORSEHAIR

After studying sculpture at university, Dahye Jeong (see also pages 97 and 158) first encountered the age-old craft of horsehair weaving through a course on her native Jeju Island, offered by the Korea Craft & Design Foundation. She adopted the technique to create baskets – a practice that earned her the Loewe Foundation Craft Prize in 2022. Following this, she was commissioned by Loewe to create a lamp for the *Loewe Lamps* exhibition at Milan Design Week 2024. The resulting work features three woven horsehair spheres encircling a central light source, casting a warm, gentle glow.

말총 조명

ANGLED BRICKS | HYUNJEE JUNG | 2024 | SILK

Created as a decorative installation for a restaurant designed by VSHD Design, this piece is a continuation of Hyunjee Jung's *Angled Bricks* series. The minimalist forms are made by folding and layering translucent fabric to create abstract geometries. For this project she uses *myeongju* – a traditional Korean silk – its diaphanous quality juxtaposed with the solidity of the brick-like forms it evokes.

기울어진 벽돌들

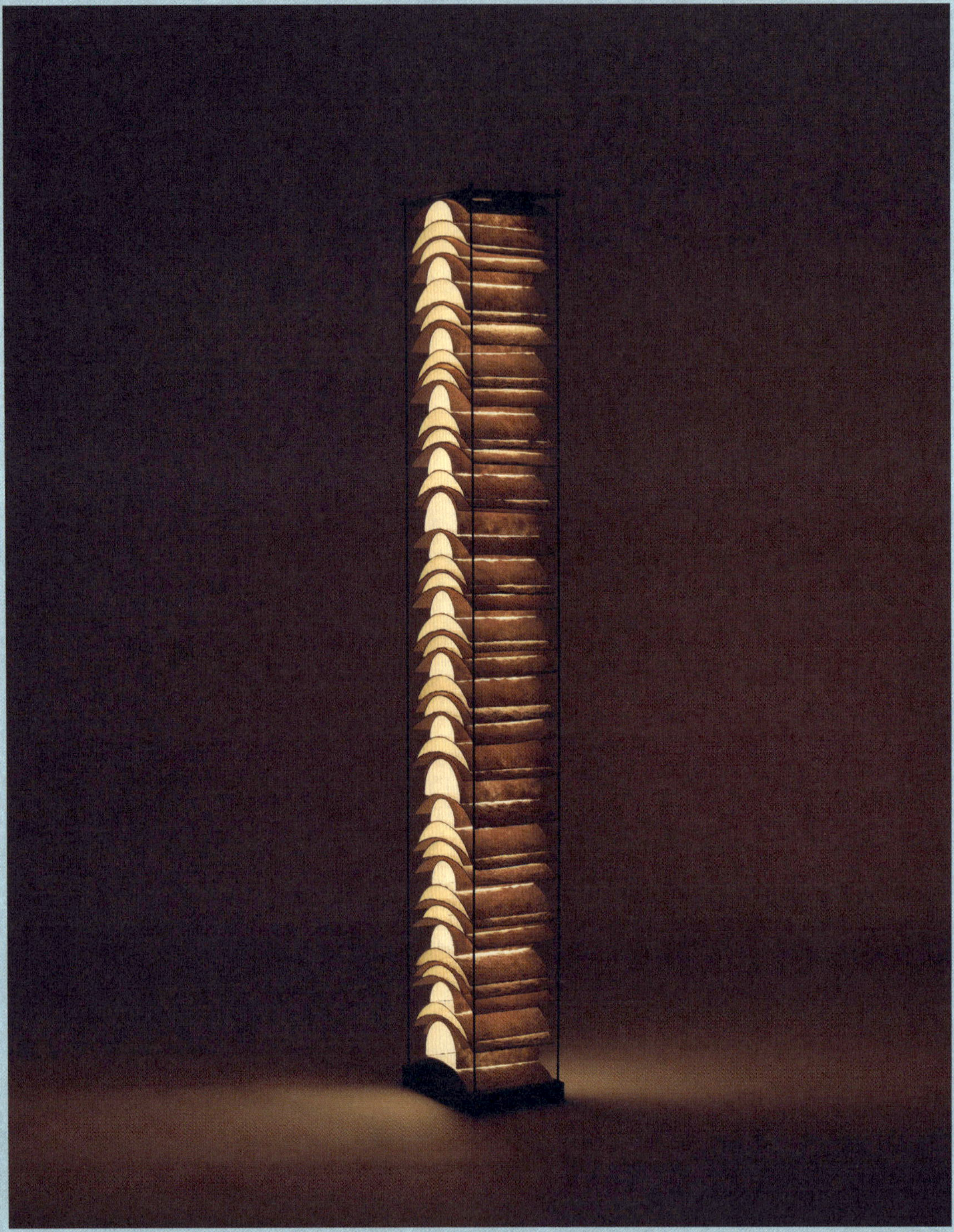

GIWA SERIES LAMP | EUNHYEON AHN | 2021 | HANJI, STEEL, LED

This floor lamp by Eunhyeon Ahn is inspired by *giwa*, the curved clay tiles used to line the roofs of traditional Korean buildings. Ahn reinterprets their distinctive form using stacked layers of *hanji* arranged along a steel frame. When lit, the paper diffuses the glow, evoking the gentle light of dusk falling over a tiled rooftop.

기와시리즈 조명

PARABOLA CHANDELIER | IL HOON ROH | 2017 | FIBRE-OPTIC CABLE, LED

Architect-turned-designer Il Hoon Roh leads his studio from Seoul, where he experiments with fibre-optic cables. The Parabola chandelier was developed through the extensive hand-weaving of luminous strands, which are strung with translucent beads to provide weight. When suspended, the cables arc into graceful parabolic curves.

파라볼라 샹들리에

LAYERS PENDANT | JUNGMO KWON | 2018 | HANJI, BRASS, LED

Lighting designer Jungmo Kwon is known for his work with *hanji*, the traditional paper that is often used in the windows and doors of *hanok*. Seeing the way *hanji* softened and scattered light in these settings inspired Kwon to incorporate it into his own designs. For these pendant lamps, he pleated the paper in concertina folds to form panels that wrap around the bulb, diffusing light with warmth and tactility.

레이어스 팬던트

NA OH LIGHTING | JUNGMO KWON | 2024 | HANJI, BRASS, LED

This sculptural light also by Jungmo Kwon (see opposite) was commissioned to hang above the tables at Na Oh, a Korean restaurant in Singapore. Also made from *hanji*, the fixture reveals a spectrum of tone, from darker areas where layers overlap to brighter sections where the paper is thin, evoking the shifting interplay of light and shadow.

나오 펜던트 조명

PIGGY BANK | ANONYMOUS | PLASTIC

This bright red plastic piggy bank (*dwaeji jeogeumtong*), with its rotund form and cartoon-like eyes, was a common sight in Korean homes from the 1970s to the 1990s. Mass-produced and inexpensive, it taught children the discipline of saving; coins went in through a slot, but often could not be retrieved without quite literally breaking the bank. In Korean culture, pigs symbolize wealth and fortune, and the colour red carries further auspicious meaning. The *dwaeji jeogeumtong* has become an enduring icon of late twentieth-century childhood.

돼지 저금통

PUNGGYEONG | ANONYMOUS | BRONZE

Traditional wind chimes, known as *punggyeong*, are often hung from the eaves of Buddhist temples in Korea. Typically made from bronze or brass, they produce a clear, resonant sound that is said to represent the voice of the Buddha and to ward off evil spirits. The clapper is commonly shaped like a fish, a symbol of happiness, abundance and – since fish never close their eyes – spiritual vigilance.

풍경

JESASANG | ANONYMOUS | JOSEON DYNASTY | VARIOUS MATERIALS

Rooted in Confucian ideals, the *jesasang* ritual table represents *hyo* (filial piety) – the duty to honour one's parents and ancestors. Set with elaborately arranged offerings of food, it links the living and the dead in a ritual of remembrance and hope. Rice and soup are placed at the centre, closest to the spirits, and a spoon is often set upright in the rice, symbolically inviting the ancestors to eat. The ritual also serves to pray for health, fortune and a good harvest.

제사상

BYEONGPUNG | ANONYMOUS | JOSEON DYNASTY | WOOD, SILK, THREAD

This is thought to be the oldest surviving example of an embroidered *byeongpung*, a Korean folding screen. Popular during the Joseon Dynasty, such screens were made by or for upper-class women and used to decorate interiors or divide rooms. This four-panel work depicts Korea's four seasons: spring flowers, summer lotus, autumn grapes, and winter plum blossom and camellia. The circular composition of the frames was unusual for the time – most were square or rectangular.

병풍

OPEN WALL | KUNSIK CHOI | 2022 | SMOKED OAK WOOD, ASH WOOD, BRASS

Open Wall is a modular screen composed of three wooden panels that can be repositioned to create varying levels of division between spaces – a contemporary response to the traditional folding screen. Central to its flexibility is an oval window in the partition, which can be adjusted to allow more or less interaction between the separated areas. Designer Kunsik Choi (see also page 129) studied industrial product design in Milan before training as a cabinetmaker in Sweden.

오픈 월

MOK GIREOGI | ANONYMOUS | JOSEON DYNASTY | WOOD

The presentation of *gireogi* (wild geese) remains a defining element of the Korean wedding ritual. Traditionally, the groom offered a live goose – which, being believed to mate for life, symbolized fidelity – to the bride's family. In time, carved wooden geese (*mok gireogi*) or ducks replaced the live ones. Typically carved from a single block of wood, they were wrapped in a red-and-blue *bojagi* (see page 98) with only their heads exposed, signifying respect and union. After the wedding, they were displayed in the home, positioned to convey the harmony of the household: beak to beak when the couple was in agreement, or tail to tail after a quarrel.

목기러기

BADUKPAN | ANONYMOUS | JOSEON DYNASTY | WOOD

The *badukpan* is the board used for *baduk* (also known as Go). This nineteenth-century example, made of pear and paulownia wood, speaks to Korea's long engagement with the game. Requiring strategy, patience and foresight, *baduk* is considered both a pastime and a discipline, echoing values deeply rooted in Korean thought.

바둑판

YUT | ANONYMOUS | WOOD

Yut refers to the four wooden sticks used in *yutnori*, a traditional board game played during Lunar New Year with an accompanying board. In mountain villages, it was once more than a game; its outcome was believed to predict the year's harvest. Villagers formed teams representing highlands and lowlands, the winning team supposedly securing the more bountiful crop yield. After the game, they would perform *mosimgi noleum*, a symbolic rice-planting ritual. Although it is no longer used for divination, the game of *yutnori* remains a beloved holiday tradition. 윷

GONGGI | ANONYMOUS | PLASTIC

공기

Gonggi, a simple game of stone-tossing that was originally played with small stones found in the streets or fields, is thought to date back to the Joseon Dynasty. Often used by children to pass the time while they waited for their parents to return home, the game involves scattering five pieces, then picking one up while tossing another into the air; it increases gradually in difficulty by collecting two, then three, and so on. As its popularity grew, the stones were replaced with brightly coloured plastic pieces, and in the early 1990s *gonggi* became a regular fixture in school playgrounds.

HWATU | ANONYMOUS | CARD

Hwatu (flower cards) is a cherished game played during Korean holidays, such as Lunar New Year and Chuseok (a celebration that is often called Korean Thanksgiving and takes place at the height of the autumn harvest). Although often dominated by members of the older generation, the game is passed down through observation and play, strengthening family bonds. It was introduced during the Japanese colonial period, but the Koreans reimagined the cards, redesigning them with vivid illustrations and creating their own rules. The cards feature such motifs as cranes, deer and moonlit scenes reflecting Korea's four seasons and its deep connection to nature.

화
투

GLOSSARY

BAEKJA
White porcelain produced during the Joseon Dynasty, associated with Confucian ideals of purity and austerity.

BAL
A bamboo blind used for shading or privacy.

BANGJJA YUGI
Hand-forged bronzeware produced using the *bangjja* technique.

BUNCHEONG
Stoneware decorated with white slip, first produced during the early Joseon Dynasty.

CHEONGJA
Celadon stoneware, distinguished by its translucent blue–green glaze, perfected during the Goryeo Dynasty.

GALDAE
Reed used in weaving and mat-making.

HANBOK
Traditional Korean dress, typically comprising a jacket (*jeogori*), skirt (*chima*) or trousers (*baji*), with variations in cut and fabric reflecting status, season and occasion.

HANJI
Handmade paper crafted from the inner bark of the mulberry tree.

HANOK
A traditional Korean house, typically built of timber, earth and stone. Usually single-storey and arranged around a courtyard.

HAP
A traditional lidded vessel used for storage or ritual offerings.

HONSU
Dowry items prepared for marriage, symbolizing a bride's household contribution.

HYO
The Confucian virtue of filial piety, embodying reverence for one's parents and ancestors.

JEONG
Difficult to translate, this Korean term refers to a deep emotional bond of affection, or attachment. Extending beyond human relationships, *jeong* can also connect people with objects, places and traditions.

JESA
A Confucian ancestral rite honouring deceased family members with offerings, typically on death anniversaries or seasonal festivals.

JISEUNG
A craft that weaves *hanji* into durable objects such as baskets, boxes and containers.

MINHWA
Korean folk art, anonymous and unsigned, created by ordinary people for daily use, ritual practice and household decoration.

MOSI
Fine ramie cloth, woven from the fibre of the Boehmeria nivea plant.

MUMYEONG
Cotton fibre, introduced to Korea in the late medieval period, which gradually replaced hemp as a staple textile.

MYEONGJU
Lustrous silk traditionally woven in Korea, used for fine clothing and ceremonial garments.

NAJEONCHILGI
Lacquerware decorated with inlaid mother-of-pearl (*najeon*).

ONDOL
An underfloor heating system using flues and heated stone.

OTTCHIL
Lacquer made from the sap of the Korean lacquer tree (*Toxicodendron vernicifluum*).

SAMBAE
Cloth woven from hemp or flax.

SEONBI
A scholar embodying Confucian ideals of integrity, modesty, and learning.

SOBAN
A small, portable wooden table used for meals and rituals.

WANGGOL
Sedge grass used in weaving mats, baskets and floor coverings.

YANGBAN
The hereditary elite of the Joseon social order, comprising civil and military officials.

KEY DATES

THREE KINGDOMS PERIOD
c. 57 BCE – 668 CE
Era of Goguryeo, Baekje and Silla, marked by rival kingdoms and the introduction of Buddhism.

UNIFIED SILLA
668 – 935
Political unification of most of the peninsula; flourishing Buddhist art and monumental temple architecture.

GORYEO DYNASTY
918 – 1392
Renowned for celadon ceramics, Buddhist printing and inlaid crafts; origin of the name 'Korea'.

JOSEON DYNASTY
1392 – 1897
Confucian state defined by refined timber architecture, white porcelain, literati painting and dress traditions later known as *hanbok*.

KOREAN EMPIRE (DAEHAN JEGUK)
1897 – 1910
Short-lived monarchy asserting sovereignty and pursuing modernization before annexation by Japan.

JAPANESE COLONIAL RULE
1910 – 1945
Period of occupation with cultural suppression alongside coerced modernization and profound social change.

DIVISION OF KOREA
1945
End of Japanese rule and partition into Soviet-administered North and US-administered South.

REPUBLIC OF KOREA (SOUTH KOREA)
1948 – present
Independent state founded in 1948; rapid modernization, industrial design and the global presence of Korean craft and culture.

DEMOCRATIC PEOPLE'S REPUBLIC OF KOREA (NORTH KOREA)
1948 – present
Separate socialist state with centrally managed cultural policy and craft production.

EDITORIAL NOTES

USE OF THE TERM 'KOREA'
Throughout the book the term 'Korea' refers to South Korea, except where clarity requires the full term 'South Korea'. 'North Korea' is used to denote the Democratic People's Republic of Korea.

ROMANIZATION OF WORDS
Korean words have been standardized according to the Official Romanization of Korean as proclaimed by the Ministry of Culture and Tourism.

FORMATTING OF NAMES
Korean names are presented according to Western conventions, with the forename preceding the surname.

INDEX

Page references in *italics* indicate images.

A

advertising fan 136, *136*
agalmatolite kettle 29, *29*
agungi (wood-fired furnace) 41, *41*
Ahn, Eunhyeon, *Giwa* series lamp 202, *202*
Ahn, Jaewoo, *Stack* cabinet 85, *85*
Amplification of Sensation chair 123, *123*
Anderson, Jonathan 13
andongpo jogakbo bojagi (patchwork cloth) 115, *115*
Angled Bricks installation 201, *201*
anseok (floor cushion) 138, *138*
Arumjigi 14–15, 161, 163

B

badukpan (game board) 212, *212*
baekja porcelain 27, 49
baguni (basket) 87, *87*
bakji technique 28
Bamgureum see Kim, Boram
bangjja yugi bowls 20, 25, *25*, 88, *88*
bangjja yugi ware 34, 35
bangseok (floor cushion) 112, 117, *117*, 143, *143*
banjikkori (sewing box) 104, *104*
banul bangseok or *banuljip* (pincushion) 95, *95*
Bauhaus 16
begaetmo (pillow end) 11, 119, *119*
beoseon (socks) 175, *175*
SoBaek slippers inspired by 160, *160*
binyeo (hairpin) 176, *176*
bitjaru (broom) 67, *67*, 68, *68*
Blessing Pouch 94, *94*
Blue Armchair 124, *124*
bojagi (wrapping cloth) 11, 98, *98*, 211
bokjumeoni (drawstring pouches) 94, *94*, 164, *164*
boryo bangseok (floor cushions) 117, *117*
Boseong Deombeongi tea bowl 48, *48*
Brass Stool 89, *89*
buchae (fans) 133, *133*, 134, *134*
Buckwheat Pillow 131, *131*
Buddhism 8, 9, 152, 207
budeul buchae (bulrush fan) 134, *134*
buncheong ware 9–10, 46, *47*
Boseong Deombeongi tea bowl 48, *48*
bottle with peonies 46, *46*
teapot with peony design 28, *28*
byeongpung (folding screen) 11, 114, *114*, 184, 209, *209*

C

Carpel series 191, *191*
Carpenters Workshop Gallery, New York 127
celadon see *cheongja*
chaeban (serving tray) 50, *50*, 99, *99*
chaekjang (storage cabinet) 78, *78*
chaesang (basket) 50, *51*, 108, *108*
chaesangjang weaving technique 108
Chang, Eungbok, *Ji-Chang* cabinet 84, *84*
chanhap (tiered food containers) 27, *27*, 30, *30*, 42, *42*, 43, *43*
cheongja (celadon) 8, 9, 52, 189, 190
hap (container) 105, *105*
mini vase 188, *188*
chimseon needlework technique 174
Cho, Eun Whan 123
Cho, Minyeol, *Expanded Fragments* no. 2 vessel 192, *192*
Cho, Sungho 13
Transition of Traces vessel 197, *197*
Choi, Dukjoo, *andongpo jogakbo bojagi* (patchwork cloth) 115, *115*
Choi, Hyung Moon 198
Choi, Jinho, *cheongja* mini vase 188, *188*
Choi, Kee Ryong, *Daam Dah* plate 199, *199*
Choi, Kunsik
Open Wall modular screen 210, *210*
W Stool 129, *129*
Chung, Yong Jin, *Side Tables With Small Facets* 59, *59*
Confucianism 8, 10, 49, 52, 64, 78, 79, 162, 175, 184, 185, 186, 208
seonbi (scholar) 64, 113, 132, 135, 163
Courtyard Vase 198, *198*
cup with handle 36, *36*
Cushion Stool (circle base) 120, *120*

D

Daam Dah plate 199, *199*
dadeumi bangmangi (laundry bats) 90, *90*
daenamu bal (woven bamboo blind) 80, *80*, 112
daeya basins 73, *73*
dalhangari see moon jar
Damyang bamboo objects 83, *83*
Daybed 141, *141*
Debaroun see Yoo, Dahyeon
dolchimdae (stone bed) 113, 137, *137*
dolsot (stone pot) 22, 22
doltap tradition 85
duru duru jumeoni (pouch) 174, *174*
dwaeji jeogeumtong (piggy bank) 206, *206*

E

ear pick 106, *106*
Eastern Edition 120
eongdeongi uija (buttocks chair) 149, 181, *181*
eun ipsa technique 100, 107
Expanded Fragments no. 2 vessel 192, *192*

F

fan 133, *133*, 134, *134*, 135, *135*, 136, *136*
fine-toothed comb 177, *177*
Floral Lattice Tray 99, *99*
Flow Bench 140, *140*
Flow leather bowl 193, *193*
Francis Gallery 130
Frost garment 161, *161*
frosted-glass bowl 23, *23*

G

galdae bitjaru *(broom)* 68, 68
gal-e-jil *woodturning technique* 140
gamasot *(cast-iron pot)* 41, 41
Garcé Dimofski 121
Gareum *lamp* 200, 200
gat *(hat)* 10–11, 13, 97, 149, 151, 151, 155
gatjip *(gat case)* 155, 155
gatot or guui *(overcoat)* 166, 166
Giwa *series lamp* 202, 202
Goguryeo tomb murals 60
gojok jeopsi *(high-footed dish)* 33, 33
gomujanggap (rubber gloves) 64, 71, *71*
gomusin (rubber shoes) 149, 180, *180*
gonggi (stone-tossing game) 185, 214, *214*
gongi (wooden pestle) 39, *39*
Goryeo Dynasty 8, 9, 52, 53, 88, 105, 106, 119, 190
Grain Cabinet 91, *91*
gulgeon (head covering) 154, *154*
gulle (headpiece) 173, *173*
gup (pedestal dish) 26, *26*
guui or *gatot* (overcoat) 166, *166*
Gwangdeok Broomcraft Studio 68
Gye, Yi Seong 8
Gyeop (Layer) screen 114, *114*

H

Ha, Jihoon 14
Haeinyo 93
Haeju hangari (jars) 81, *81*
hahoetal (wooden mask) 156, *156*
hanbok (traditional dress) 15, 90, 126, 148, 149, 157, 161, 164, 172, 174, 175, 178
hangari (jar) 52, *52*, 81, *81*
Hanging Split no. 247 (hanging textile) 116, *116*
hanji paper 9, 58, 65, 82, 84, 91, 103, 135, 138, 151, 155, 172, 202, 204, 205
hanji basket 82, *82*
hanok (traditional house) 14, 15, 41, 76, 112, 139, 142
hap (lidded containers) 54, *54*, 93, *93*, 105, *105*
hapjukseon (bamboo fan) 135, *135*
Hohodang 98, *98*
Huh, Sangwook, *buncheong* teapot with peony design 28, *28*
Hur, Sung Ja, *Married Couple bangseok* (floor cushion) 143, *143*
hwagakam (storage box) 101, *101*
hwamunseok (floor mat) 145, *145*
Hwang, Han Gap, *kkotsin* (silk shoes) 172, *172*

hwarot (ceremonial robe) 149, 165, *165*
hwatu (flower cards) 215, *215*
Hyu Chair 125, *125*
hyungbae (silk badge) 11, 178, *178*

I

Im, Jungjoo, *Flow Bench* 140, *140*
Inborn Ott-003 194, *194*
incense burner 190, *190*

J

jagaejang (lacquered cabinet) 65, 74, *74*
jangot (overcoat) 162, *162*
Jari mat 145, *145*
jeolgu (mortar) 39, *39*
Jeon, Seong Im
Blessing Pouch 94, *94*
The Sound of Spring basket 109, *109*
Jeong, Dahye 13
Gareum lamp 200, *200*
norigae (pendant) 158, *158*
A Time of Sincerity basket 97, *97*
Jeong, Eun Mi, *malgun* (over-garment) 169, *169*
jeongja (small wooden pavilion) 112–13, 132, *132*
jeongjagwan (indoor hat) 150, *150*
jesa (ancestral rites) 26, 54, 184
jesasang (ritual table) 184, 208, *208*
Ji-Chang cabinet 84, *84*
jige (carrying frame) *77*, *77*
jipsin (sandals) 159, *159*
jiseung technique 58, 65, 82, 138
jiseungban table 58, *58*
jiseungham (paper cord boxes) 65
jitaechilgi storage box 103, *103*
Jo, Hyung Suk, *Daybed* 141, *141*
jokduri (headpiece) 149
Joseon Dynasty 8, 9–10, 17, 65, 113, 184
bronzeware 35, 42
carpets 144
clothing 150–55, 162–63, 165–66, 169, 171–74, 176–79
fans 134–35
furniture 56, 58, 74, 75, 78, 79, 84, 141, 208, 209
games 212, 214
lacquerware 96
masks 156
pillows 119
porcelain 27, 31, 33, 45, 49, 52, 185, 186, 187
rituals 211
silverware 100
stoneware 29, 46, 48, 81
storage boxes 30, 42, 54, 93, 101, 104, 107
weaving techniques 86, 97
jukbuin (body pillow) 112, 122, *122*
Jung, Hyunjee, *Angled Bricks* installation 201, *201*

K

Kang, Suk Keun 13
ottchil wooden bowl 102, *102*
ki (grain sieve) 37, *37*
Kim, Boram (Bamgureum)
Floral Lattice Tray 99, *99*
Square Tea Basket 92, *92*
Kim, Chanhyeok, low desk (*CHim* series) 139, *139*
Kim, Christina
Frost garment 161, *161*
norigae (pendant) 157, *157*
Kim, Dong Jun, moon jar 187, *187*
Kim, Eun Hak, *Grain Cabinet* 91, *91*
Kim, Gwang Gyun 168
Kim, Hyejeong 14
Oriental Moon pot 191, *191*
Kim, Hyun Sung, *Brass Stool* 89, *89*
Kim, Il Woong, *Three-Tiered Chanhap* 42, *42*
Kim, Jinsik, *Soften* coffee table 128, *128*
Kim, Joo Young 198
Kim, Junsu, *Flow* leather bowl 193, *193*
Kim, Kyung Hee, *jeongjagwan* (indoor hat) 150, *150*
Kim, Minjae, *Lacquered Chairs* 121, *121*
Kim, Minwook, *Pruning* vessel 195, *195*
Kim, Sangin
gojok jeopsi (high-foot dish) 33, *33*
small *hap* 93, *93*
Unmun bowl and plate 31, *31*
Kim, Seon Hui 168
Kim, Sooyon, *Hanging Split no. 247* (hanging textile) 116, *116*
Kim, Sun Tae, lidded bowl with two handles 43, *43*
Kim, Sunjin 131, 160
Kim, Young Eun, *duru duru*
jumeoni (pouch) 174, *174*
kkotsin (silk shoes) 149, 172, *172*
Korea Craft & Design Foundation 200
Korean Heritage Room, University of Pittsburgh 14
Kwon, Jungmo
Layers pendant 204, *204*
Na Oh lighting 205, *205*
Kwon, Won Deok
Grain Cabinet 91, *91*
Hyu Chair 125, *125*

L

Lacquered Chairs 121, *121*
Layers pendant 204, *204*
Lee, Dong Kyun, *galdae bitjaru* (broom) 68, *68*
Lee, Gee Jo, *chanhap* (tiered food container) 27, *27*
Lee, Inchin 14
Lee, Jaiik, *Transition_Irregular Rhythm* vessel 196, *196*
Lee, Jong Duk
bangjja bowl 88, *88*
low lidded bowl 34, *34*
spoon & chopstick set 35, *35*
Lee, Jung Hoon, *saeksilnubi* pincushion 95, *95*
Lee, Kang Hyo, *Oval Bottle* 47, *47*
Lee, Kwangho, *Blue Armchair* 124, *124*
Lee, Kyung Sun
guui (overcoat) 166, *166*
King Yeongjo's *dopo* (robe) 163, *163*
Lee, Seung Yeon, frosted-glass bowl 23, *23*
Lee, Yesl
boryo bangseok (floor cushion) 117, *117*
Gyeop (Layer) screen 114, *114*
Sambal table 60, *60*
lidded bowl with two handles 43, *43*
Lim, Seoyoon 131, 160
Limn Seoul 116
Loewe Foundation Craft Prize 13, 200
Low Desk (*CHim* series) 139, *139*
low lidded bowl 34, *34*
Lyu, Namgwon, *jitaechilgi* storage box 103, *103*

M

maetdol (stone mill) 40, *40*
Maezm, *Amplification of Sensation* chair 123, *123*
majokban table 56, *56*
malgun (over-garment) 169, *169*
Married Couple bangseok (floor cushion) 143, *143*
Metropolitan Museum of Art, New York 47
Milan Design Week 200
mingei movement 10
minhwa aesthetic 81
modam (carpet) 144, *144*
Mohm
beoseon slippers 160, *160*
Buckwheat Pillow 131, *131*
mok gireogi (carved wooden geese) 211, *211*
mokchim (headrest) 119
moon jar (*dalhangari*) 185, 186, *186*, 187, *187*, 196
mother-of-pearl inlay 10, 65, 74, 96, 119
mul ot (water clothing) 170, *170*
mumi philosophy 17
myeokseori (straw container) 69, *69*

N

Na Oh lighting 205, *205*
najeon-chilgi sewing box 96, *96*
Naju Bansang tables 14
norigae (pendant) 157, *157*, 158, *158*
nubi jeogori (quilted jacket) 167, *167*

O

Obsession series 124, *124*
oil bottle 53, *53*
ondol (floor-heating system) 10, 112, 137, 138, 142
onggi (earthenware jar) 20–21, 38, *38*
Onjium 14, 15, 60, 117, 161, 163, 166
Open Wall modular screen 210, *210*
Oriental Moon pot 191, *191*
ottchil technique 13, 103, 193, 194
ottchil wooden bowl 102, *102*
Oval Bottle 47, *47*

P

Parabola Chandelier 203, *203*
parichae (plastic fly swatter) 70, *70*
Park, Seo Hee, *Polygonal Container* 189, *189*

Park, Sung Youl, *Inborn Ott-003* 194, *194*
Park, Wonmin, *Plain Cuts Box Chair* 127, *127*
Park, Young Mi, *hanji* basket 82, *82*
Plain Cuts Box Chair 127, *127*
Polygonal Container 189, *189*
Porventura 128
ppallaepan (washing board) 66, *66*
Projekt Produkt 129
Pruning vessel 195, *195*
Pulzip Craft Museum, Gwangju 86, 94, 109
punggyeong (wind chime) 207, *207*

R

Roh, Il Hoon, *Parabola Chandelier* 203, *203*
Ryu, Yeunhee 14

sabangtakja (display shelf) 79, *79*
saeksilnubi pincushion 95, *95*
salchang gojaengi (undergarment) 171, *171*
Sambal table 60, *60*
samcheungjang (three-tiered chest) 75, *75*
sangbo (square cloth) 44, *44*
sangbok (mourning clothes) 154
sanggam inlay technique 9, 199
sangmo (rice straw hat) 153, *153*
sangtugwan (hairpin) 179, *179*
satgat (bamboo hat) 152, *152*
Seo, Han Gyu 51
Seo, Sin Jeong, *chaesang* (black-lacquered basket) 51, *51*
seonbi (Confucian scholar) 64, 113, 132, 135, 163
seonbi jeongsin (*seonbi* spirit) 64
Shin, Sunyi 14
Shin, Tai Ho 123
Shon, Shinkyu, *SPLIT* series 76, *76*
Side Table 130, *130*
Side Tables With Small Facets 59, *59*
silver inlaid vessel 100, *100*
small *hap* 93, *93*
SoBaek slippers 160, *160*
soban (table) 10, *56*, *56–59*, *57*, *58*, 139
Soften coffee table 128, *128*
sokuri (basket) 32, *32*
Soluna Living
Jari mat 145, *145*
wanggol hwabangseok (floor cushion) 142, *142*
somok joinery technique 92, 125
Song, Gi Jin, *Boseong Deombeongi* tea bowl 48, *48*
The Sound of Spring basket 109, *109*
SPLIT series 76, *76*
spoon and chopstick set 35, *35*
Square Tea Basket 92, *92*
Stack cabinet 85, *85*
Studio Millionroses, *Courtyard Vase* 198, *198*

T

Taiping Laoren 9
Tang Dynasty China 96
Three Kingdoms period 36, 38, 96, 102, 157, 175
Three-Tiered Chanhap 42, *42*
A Time of Sincerity basket 97, *97*
tobacco boxes 107, *107*
Tone side tables 126, *126*
Transition of Traces vessel 197, *197*
Transition_Irregular Rhythm vessel 196, *196*
ttaesugeon (exfoliating towel) 64, 72, *72*
tteoksal (rice cake stamp) 55, *55*
ttukbaegi earthenware 20

U

Unmun bowl and plate 31, *31*

V

Victoria & Albert Museum, London 47, 189
VSHD Design 201

W

W Stool 129, *129*
wanggol baskets 109
wanggol hwabangseok (floor cushion) 142, *142*
wedding bedding set 118, *118*
white porcelain bottles 45, *45*, 49, *49*
wonban (round table) 31, 57, *57*
wonsam (ceremonial robe) 149, 168, *168*
Woo, Hee, bamboo *baguni* (basket) 87, *87*
Woven Leather Case 86, *86*

Y

Yanagi, Sōetsu 10
Yang, Byung Yong
majokban table 56, *56*
wonban (round table) 57, *57*
Yang, Teo 36
Cushion Stool (circle base) 120, *120*
yangeun bowls 21, 24, *24*
yangeun naembi aluminium pots 21
Yeongjo, King, *dopo* (robe) 163, *163*
yeot scissors 61, *61*
yeoyu concept 112, 113
yo (quilted bedding) 65
Yoo, Bae Geun, *Grain Cabinet* 91, *91*
Yoo, Dahyeon (Debaroun), *Woven Leather Case* 86, *86*
Yoon, Rahee, *Side Table* 130, *130*
Youonejae Hot Spring Hotel, Chungbuk Province 125
Yun, Sohyun, *Tone* side tables 126, *126*
yut (*yutnori* sticks) 213, *213*
yutnori (game) 184, 213

IMAGE CREDITS

Every effort has been made to trace the copyright holders and obtain permission to reproduce this material. The publisher apologizes for any errors or omissions and would be grateful if notified of any corrections that should be incorporated in future reprints or editions of this book.

ABASK: 82, 87, 88; Arumjigi Foundation: 41; Arumjigi Foundation, © Guru Visual: 42, 43, 60, 114, 117, 139, 141, 157, 161, 166, 169; Bamgureum (Boram Kim): 92, 99; Bangim Craft: 56, 57; Daria Arnautova / Alamy Stock Photo: 24; Dukjoo Choi: 115; Eastern Edition: 120; Eunkyung Kim: 195; courtesy Gallery LVS: 187; photo by Gangjinju: 22, 25; courtesy Goldmark Gallery: 47; courtesy Hohodang: 98; Hur Sung Ja: 143; Hyejeong Kim: 191; Ivo Oliveira Rodrigues: 128; Jaewoo Ahn: 85; Jang Soo In: 198; Jung Hoon Lee: 95; Jung Joo Im: 140; Jung Mo Kwon: 204; KC Studio: 59, 193; Korea Heritage Service: 108; Kang Jinju: 205; Kim Jan Dee: 89; Kim Kwonjin: 129; © Koo Bon Chang: 50, 69; Korean Craft and Design Foundation: 90; Kun Sik Choi: 210; Kwangchoon Park: 196, 197; Leeum Museum of Art: 45, 46; Limn Seoul: 116; Living Sense: 51; MAEZM: 123; Mohm: 131, 160; Mono Collection: 84; Namgwon Lyu: 103; National Folk Museum of Korea: 40, 55, 58, 61, 122, 134, 135, 136, 152, 154, 156, 159, 164, 167, 175, 176, 177, 178, 179, 212, 215; National Museum of Korea: 49, 106, 186, 190; National Palace Museum of Korea: 208; Oculis Project: 201; courtesy ONJIUM Research Institute for Korean Cultural Heritage, © Guru Visual: 163; Onyang Folk Museum: 29, 44, 54, 96, 100, 101, 104, 153, 155, 162, 170, 171, 211, 213; Pulzip Craft Musuem: 94, 109; Salon 94 Design: 124; © Sean Davidson: 121; Seohee Park: 189; Seoul Museum of Craft Art: 105, 144, 150, 151, 165, 168, 172, 173, 209; Shannon Tofts: 199; Shinkyu Shon: 76; Shutterstock: 214; Sohyun Yun: 126; Sol Kwon: 86; SOLUNA FINE CRAFT: 28, 83, 97, 142, 145, 158, 200; Sooin Jang: 130; Studio Il Hoon Roh: 203; Studio Kō Los Angeles: 23, 68, 174, 188, 202; Studio Mark I: 194; Courtesy Studio Tashtego, photography by Jeff Mikkelson: 192; Suk Keun Kang: 102; Thitaporn Santipolvut / Alamy Stock Photo: 207; © Victoria and Albert Museum, London: 52, 53, 107; Won Deok Kwon: 91, 125; Wonmin Park, © Thomas Chene: 127

commissioned photography: © Hyunwoo Min: 30, 31, 32, 33, 34, 35, 36, 37, 38, 39, 66, 67, 70, 71, 72, 73, 74, 75, 77, 78, 79, 80, 81, 93, 118, 119, 132, 133, 138, 180, 181, 206

ACKNOWLEDGEMENTS

The publisher would like to express deep gratitude to the many individuals who helped realise this project. The publication would not have been possible without the support of, and contributions from, the following:

Arumjigi
Beth McKillop
Emma Caddy
Ibi Yoo of Studio Kō
J Kathryn Hong
Je Seung Lee
Leeum Museum of Art
National Folk Museum of Korea
Onjium
Onyang Folk Museum
Rachel Sampson
Rosanna Fairhead
Seoul Museum of Craft Art
Soluna Fine Craft
Teo Yang
Victoria & Albert Museum

Our sincere thanks go to the many designers and craftspeople who have been generous with their time and contributions, as well as to Hester Underhill for her assistance in researching and writing several of the project texts. We are also deeply grateful to Hyunwoo Min for his beautiful photography, featured throughout and shot on location specifically for this book.

The author wishes to extend special thanks to Nolan Giles, without whom this book would simply not exist.

AUTHOR BIOS

HYO JUNG LEE is a Korean-born graphic designer based in London. In 2020, she founded the *Korean Craft and Design* digital platform, through which she has facilitated dialogues between Korean and international designers to explore how leading creatives draw inspiration from Korea's craft culture. She has spent her career working with international branding agencies and is currently at Pentagram.

BETH MCKILLOP was formerly curator of Chinese and Korean collections at the British Library and Deputy Director of the Victoria & Albert Museum (2011-2016), where she is currently a senior research fellow. She was president of the Oriental Ceramic Society (2018-2021) and co-authored *Precious beyond Measure: A History of Korean Ceramics* published in 2024.

J KATHRYN HONG has served as the Chief Creative Officer of Onjium, guiding research and dissemination efforts focused on Korea's traditional culture of food, clothing and housing, since 2013. In 2025, she was appointed Chairperson of the Arumjigi Foundation – a non-profit private organization that showcases the beauty and values of traditional Korean culture.

TEO YANG is the founder of Teo Yang Studio, known for designing commercial and high-end residential projects and creative collaborations with international luxury brands. His studio earned the prestigious AD100 award from *Architectural Digest* in 2022 and was shortlisted for Dezeen's Interior Designer of the Year award in 2024. Teo Yang has also launched his own furniture brand Eastern Edition and skincare brand EATH Library.

Phaidon Press Limited
2 Cooperage Yard
London E15 2QR

Phaidon Press Inc.
111 Broadway
New York, NY 10006

Phaidon SARL
55, rue Traversière
75012 Paris

phaidon.com

ISBN 978 1 83866 945 4

A CIP catalogue record for this book is available from the British Library and the Library of Congress.

Commissioning Editor: Joe Pickard
Production Controller: Rebecca Price
Additional texts: Hester Underhill
Commissioned photography: Hyunwoo Min
Design: Julia Hasting
Artworking: Cantina

Printed in China

phaidon.com

978 1 83866 945 4